BENOÎT PIÉRON

Slumber Party

'The few pages which follow ... draw their entire strength from the fact that the story is completely true since I made it up from beginning to end. Its material realisation – to use the correct expression – consists basically of a projection of reality, under favourable circumstances, on to [*sic*] an irregularly tilting, and consequently distorting, plane of reference.'
–Boris Vian, *Froth on the Daydream*.[1]

Z
INTRODUCTION
É

W
H
I
T
L
E
Y

Boris Vian closes the foreword to his tragically surreal novel *L'Écume des jours* (1947). Anglophone translators disagree on whether to call it *Froth on the Daydream*, *Mood Indigo*, or *Foam of the Daze*, a bizarre yet fitting lack of consensus for an allegorical work that is hard to summarise and even harder to pin down. In Vian's story, a water lily blooms in the right lung of a main character, prefiguring an insurmountable illness and the precariousness of day-to-day living. Absolute truth consisting of authored fabrication. A skewed manipulation through which to see everyday circumstances more clearly. Encompassing a truly kaleidoscopic range of reference points, Vian's words hold equally true for Benoît Piéron's Chisenhale Gallery commission. *Slumber Party* is a hazy hallucination, a patchwork of harshness cloaked in happiness, based on actual events.

I ‘met’ Piéron for the first time in December 2021, whilst conducting a virtual studio visit. Nearly two years later, the artist is presenting his first solo exhibition in the United Kingdom, illustrating our commitment to working closely with artists who develop their ideas over a period of eighteen to twenty-four months. Benoît's CV immediately struck me, as it was as much a hospital record as a tally of exhibitions and residencies. Born with meningitis in 1983, the artist has had illness as his lifelong companion, survival his raison d'être. Conversant – I'd go so far as to say fluent – in English and Spanish alongside his native French, he has heartrendingly described to us at Chisenhale Gallery how his mother tongue is pain.

PIÉRON was one of precious few survivors to overcome the contaminated-blood scandal that rocked France and reverberated around the world, in which medical professionals administered HIV-positive blood transfusions to patients, including a young Piéron. As one of only two children at his local hospital to pull through this catastrophe, the artist now has a creative trajectory inextricably entwined with his journeys away from and towards salubrity. For decades, from his many places of convalescence, Piéron has commanded the power of dreaming, of travelling without necessarily moving. The visions that materialise are summoned from the artist's imagination both as a means to forestall pain and under the aegis of literal painkillers.

WE are inspired by the exciting and thought-provoking ways in which artists reinterpret the world, and Chisenhale's commissions allow us to share those visions publicly. Piéron is an exemplar of transformational world-building. His expression is singular, yet he doesn't work in isolation. His works emerge from the joy and agony that blossom in the fertile ground of shared lived experience and crafty hands. It was my tremendous honour and responsibility to translate the artist-to-artist conversation between Piéron and Chisenhale trustee Paul Maheke. What a privilege to listen to their original, unfiltered exchange, garnering the artist's stamp of approval for being neither blunt nor smoothed out in English. Artists speaking to other artists is the form of art writing I personally most enjoy reading, and credit is due to coeditor and Associate Curator Amy Jones for a careful condensation of a deliciously lengthy interview that retains both marrow and soul.

C
O
M
M
I
S
S
I
O
N
S

Curator Olivia Aherne has ably led Chisenhale's skilful and dedicated team, including ever-ingenious Head Technician Lucy Woodhouse; Asymmetry Curatorial Research Fellow Rachel Be-Yun Wang; Other People's Sculpture, fabricators of the exhibition's sculptural elements; Charles Stanton-Jones and Christopher MacInnes, providers of lighting expertise; Aneeka Makwana, whose care-laden stitching complements Piéron's own; and Coppermill Ltd, for supplying the UK hospital sheets that have made their way into the patchwork of the artist's oeuvre. We take neither our collaborators' time nor their work for granted.

I

likewise extend gratitude to those who brought playfulness and thoughtfulness to the pages of this book, including contributors Paul Maheke, Clay AD, and Roxanne Maillet. Thank you to this publication's assistant editor, Terra Foundation Curatorial Fellow Oscar Abdulla. The book design by Gloria Favaro sensitively translates Piéron's outlook to the printed page. The realisation of this publication is made possible through the generous support of our Lead Supporter, Fondation Pernod Ricard, and our Headline Supporters, Fluxus Art Projects and The Clare McKeon Charitable Trust with additional thanks to the Chisenhale Gallery Publishing Supporters' Circle, and Galerie Sultana.

Chisenhale Commissions Fund members are essential to every project's realisation: Shane Akeroyd, the Cingilli Collection, Emma & Fred Goltz, Fabiana Marenghi Vaselli Bond, Patrizia Memmo, Mato Perić, Bianca Roden, Matthew Slotover and Emily King, Andreas Teoh, and Ms Yan Du.

Lead Exhibition Supporter: Fondation Pernod Ricard.

Headline Supporters: Fluxus Art Projects, The Clare McKeon Charitable Trust, and Galerie Sultana.

With additional thanks to Chisenhale Gallery Publishing Supporters' Circle.

Chisenhale Gallery's Public Programme 2023 is supported by the Talks & Events Supporters Circle.

Chisenhale Gallery's Schools' Programme 2023 is made possible through the generosity of Headline Supporter Goodman Gallery.

The Chisenhale Gallery Curatorial Fellowship 2023–24 is supported by the Terra Foundation for American Art.

The 2023–24 Asymmetry Curatorial Research Fellow is hosted by Chisenhale Gallery.

1 Boris Vian, *Froth on the Daydream*, trans. Stanley Chapman (London: Penguin Books, 1970), 7.

Let the Slumber Party commence!

AN INTERLUDE

OLIVIA AHERNE

Waiting is generally considered a frustrating waste of time, but for Benoît Piéron, it is an opportunity – political, creative, imaginative. This publication brings together a community of voices, some familiar to Piéron and others soon to become so. Much like the artist's own approach of stitching together discarded materials – predominantly used and stained hospital sheets – this book threads together contributions from artists and collaborators to create a collective corpus that speaks to illness, feels pain, and invites you to wait with them a while. Through conversation and design, Benoît Piéron, Clay AD, Gloria Favaro, Paul Maheke, and Roxanne Maillet take the waiting room as context, and the slumber party as intervention.

Deliberately mirroring the format of a waiting-room magazine, large-format, full-bleed images and glossy spreads become imaginary portals through which to journey. A series of commissioned activities, unproductive in nature, interrupt the book's contents, inviting the reader to fall out of sync, change gears, or circle back – a dragging out and looping back of time onto itself. Through a provocation to make origami, Piéron solicits a literal tearing out and folding of pages, an undoing and collapsing of the book's own chronology and manifestation. Time bends here, liberating us from linear, progressive, normative experience.

While Piéron's Chisenhale Gallery commission draws together the two contexts in which he is working – the UK and France – via used cotton hospital sheets that once lined their beds, Clay AD's textual contribution continues a journey into the waiting room, articulating experiences across its times, spaces, and bodies. Zoé Whitley's text weaves together a patchwork of voices and literary references from which Piéron's practice emerges, while a conversation between Piéron and Paul Maheke traverses artistic process and institutional relations.

From behind the cubicle curtain, the book journeys through the artist's studio and reveals early sketches of the commission. Conversation, collaboration, and making together become centerfolds. In the waiting-room magazine, if one takes the time to look, a different reality is revealed. At the intersection of sleep and waiting, and within the pages of this book, a slumber party can be found. In this space of liminality and suspended time, waiting and uncertainty become opportunities to dream together.

BENOÎT PIÉRON: A PATCHWORK FOR DREAMING AWAKE

ZOÉ WHITLEY

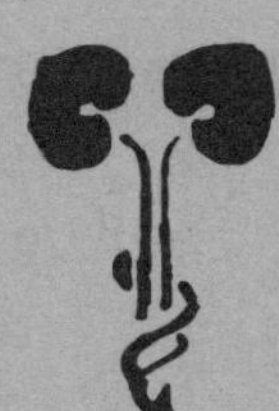

‘After all, is there any person so unhappy, so abandoned, that he doesn’t have a little den into which he can withdraw and hide away from everyone? Nothing more elaborate is needed for the journey.’
–Xavier de Maistre, *A Journey around My Room* (1794).[1]

‘I would sleep for a few hours and then I would get up, go to the john, write down my dreams on little scraps of paper without my glasses, take two aspirin, do my hand exercises, spider-crawling up the wall of the bathroom, and then go back to bed for another few hours and some more dreams.’
–Audre Lorde, *The Cancer Journals* (1980).[2]

‘People would say, “Can I come to your studio?” And, I’d say, “Sure, but my studio is underneath my bed.”’
–Felix Gonzalez-Torres (1995).[3]

p. 13
Benoît Piéron, *Le Lit* (2010). Installation view, General Stores, Pantin, 2022.
Photo: Origins Studio. Courtesy of Fondation d’entreprise Hermès.

Slumber Party is an autobiografictional utopia. As with the selected quotes above, Benoît Piéron patchworks diaristic lived experience, journeys through a rich interior landscape, and resonant art historical references. Like the canopy overhead as you enter his Chisenhale Gallery commission, what follows is a patchwork of references that speak to his conceptual universe. It is a constellation that originates from an axiom of human existence: our bodies will fail us. None of us are immune from pain or illness, sometimes chronic. Living and death are inescapably conjoined human realities. Audre Lorde referred to this fact when she wrote, ‘The only answer to death is the heat and confusion of living.’[4] It’s no wonder that the cultural and literary influences Piéron holds most dear each possessed a remarkable ability to face premature death hastened by illness or incident.

‘Being alive is a risk’, observed Anne Dufourmantelle (1964–2017).[5] A psychoanalyst and contemporary philosopher, Dufourmantelle lived this dictum to her own dying breath, risking and ultimately giving her life trying to rescue two drowning children. The inevitability of loss, of suffering, permeates Piéron’s oeuvre with a disconcerting levity. The artist smuggles life’s harsher yet inevitable truths into loving stitches, alluring colours, and cuddly, covetable objects. He refers to this strategy as radical softness.

Radical softness, an intentional clash of opposites, suggests a gentleness that persists in the face of otherwise brutal or hopeless conditions. Unlike the ‘soft life’ of languor and leisure, free of hardship, subversion comes from seeking what soothes and finding joy in circumstances where despair or despondency are understandable responses. It calls to mind the photograph on the Penguin paperback cover of Derek Jarman’s *At Your Own Risk* (1992), of a freshly laundered shirt billowing in a harsh wind.[6] Below the washing line, poppies thrive among the rocky and seemingly inhospitable stretches of shingle where Jarman made his warm and peaceful home at Prospect Cottage in Dungeness, Kent. (The area has become an unlikely place of emblematic softness, a rich biodiversity where boiling wastewater from the local nuclear power plant nurtures a fertile seabed ecosystem for fish and birds.)

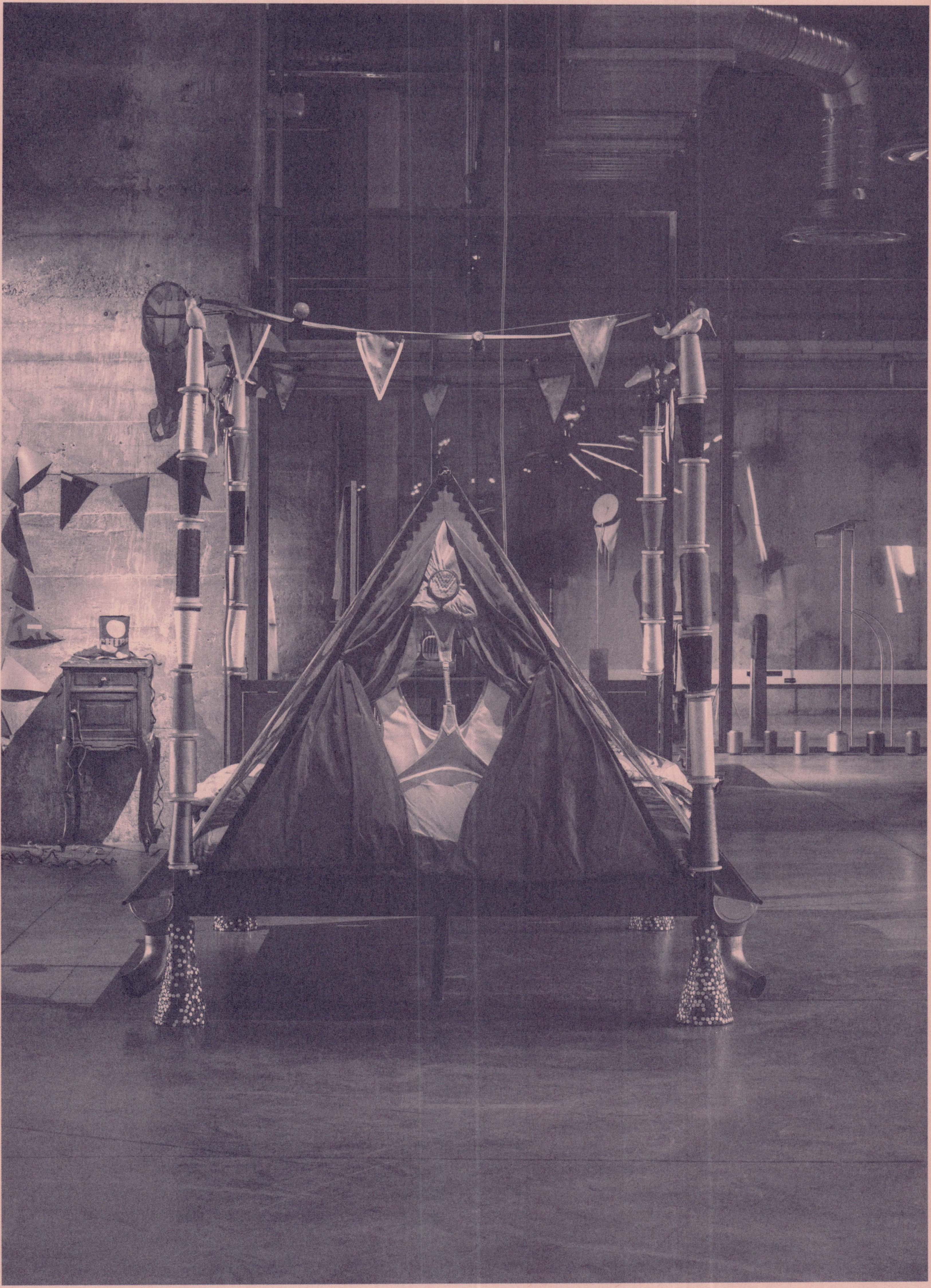

Like Felix Gonzalez-Torres (1957–1996), who used curtains, candies, billboards, clocks, and lightbulbs, Piéron injects meaning into recognisable objects. The highly subjective merges with the expansively indeterminate. Both artists are known collectors of toys, suggesting a certain literal playfulness but also an intact sense of wonder about the world. Gonzalez-Torres proudly collapsed the boundaries between artist and work to actively include the viewer. He challenged the very notion of what might be considered art, and rejected value and meaning as bedfellows of rarity. He also showed us that art could be replenishable, well-stocked rather than scarce. In sum, he made work that attempts to capture what it means to be alive. He referred to himself using the medical term 'infiltrator' – a self-perceptive superpower whereby he could access, then alter, the surrounding norms.[7]

Writing from the specificity of post-mastectomy breast cancer, Lorde articulated the 'commonality of isolation and painful reassessment' that can be applied to serious illness generally. She also spoke collectively of those who 'not without fear, have survived cancer by scrutinising its meaning within our lives, and by attempting to integrate this crisis into useful strengths for change.'[8] This leads to a question central to Piéron: how to participate in society while also finding a means to comfort oneself away from it. The answer is found, necessarily, in creating a refuge. Piéron's *Le Lit* (2010) is an artwork-cum-resting-place where invitingly soft bedding provides not only rest but also comforts, including beverages and toast. For Absalon, the professional alias of the Israeli French artist Meir Eshel (1964–1993), whose work was shown at Chisenhale Gallery posthumously in 1995 following his death from HIV-related complications, the retreat and personal domain were one, resulting in his bespoke sculptural units called *cellules* (cells), based on his own biometrics: 'I would like to create my own setting and belong to nothing else [...]. My homeland will be in between them.'[9]

Beyond the fabrication of purely functional rooms for living, Piéron makes space for loving and dreaming. As Gonzalez-Torres observed, 'You need that space, you need that lifting up, you need that traveling in your mind that love brings, transgressing the limits of your body and your imagination.'[10] To make 'life more drinkable for the dreamers', as Piéron intends, he also refuses to deny the ill body the capacity of and desire for the emotional and physical pleasures of attraction, love, and sex.[11] Bed is not only for sleeping or convalescing.

Piéron embodies Gustav Metzger's encouraging dictum: 'Art, I believe, needs to sink into the centre of a human being, come up, and that will be hope – the art will be hope. The art will have the energy and the wisdom out of the deep entering into oneself and into nature.'[12] A slumber party is a wonderful contradiction – ostensibly a gathering at night to sleep communally, but designed to reward those who can fend off drowsiness and greet the dawning of a bright new day together. Ultimately, Benoît Piéron's art gives form to vulnerability without hopelessness.

1 Xavier de Maistre, *A Journey around My Room*, trans. Andrew Brown (Richmond, London: Alma Classics, 2017), 3.
2 Audre Lorde, *The Cancer Journals* (San Francisco: spinsters|aunt lute, 1980), 52.
3 Ross Bleckner, 'Felix Gonzalez-Torres', *BOMB* 51 (April 1995): https://bombmagazine.org/articles/felix-gonzalez-torres/.
4 Lorde, *The Cancer Journals*, 47.
5 Anastasia Vécrin, 'Interview: Anne Dufourmantelle', *Libération*, September 14, 2015, https://www.liberation.fr/debats/2015/09/14/anne-dufourmantelle-la-securite-engendre-plus-la-peur-quel-inverse_1382441/.
6 Derek Jarman, *At Your Own Risk* (London: Penguin Vintage Classics, 2019).
7 Bleckner, 'Felix Gonzalez-Torres'.
8 Lorde, *The Cancer Journals*, 10.
9 Susanne Pfeffer, *Absalon* (Tel Aviv: Tel Aviv Museum of Art, 2013), 181.
10 Bleckner, 'Felix Gonzalez Torres'.
11 Liverpool Biennial, 'Benoît Piéron', June 2023, https://www.biennial.com/artists/benoit-pieron/.
12 Emma Ridgway, 'Interview | Gustav Metzger', *RSA Arts and Ecology* (April 2009): https://archive.ph/Iu6a.

A CONVERSATION: BENOÎT PIÉRON AND PAUL MAHEKE

TRANSLATED BY

ZOÉ WHITLEY

PAUL MAHEKE
I first came across your work at the end of 2021 through our gallerist, Guillaume Sultana at Galerie Sultana. I'm always fascinated by where an artist finds their beginnings – how they arrive at art and decide what will accompany them on their life's journey. So I'd like to start by asking how your relationship with art began.

BENOÎT PIÉRON
The start, for me, was when I was about six years old. At that time, I was being treated for leukaemia, for which I underwent a three-year course of chemotherapy. As a result, there were very few days when I could go to school, and I became an anthropologist of sorts, an explorer of the exotic world of the non-disabled.

When I did go to school, I didn't understand the behavioural codes. My everyday was life or death, so the rest didn't register. There was a very charismatic, but equally violent, little girl who would intercept me in the stairwell because I was different from the others. One day, I brought to school a game I'd created. I'd made characters, little artefacts, on a grid and invented rules. That was my first piece. I'd created a playground, a safe space for myself so I could navigate a place I otherwise couldn't fully comprehend. The little girl loved the game, and after that she kind of became my protector queen / mafia godfather!

P
M

[*laughs*] You know, it's also true for me that art serves as a pretext for an encounter. Do you recall when you decided this would guide your adult life?

B
P

My artistic practice was nourished by an initial trauma, so there's a biographical element to it. I didn't necessarily associate my art with that event, at first. It took being back in hospital to return to that first trauma, to be reliving situations that I then understood to be what I was attempting to give materiality to. My artistic practice is a ventriloquism for malady; it coexists with my internal landscape.

P
M

In that sense, illness is not only a subject of your work but also its own means of production.

B
P

Yes. It's an energy in Donna Haraway's sense: a compost.[1] It's combustible. The idea of what could destroy me also nourished me – economically, humanly. In terms of interrelation, it's my contact zone – like human skin, simultaneously interior and exterior. My question is always whether people perceive my work as an internalisation or an externalisation? As long as I haven't answered that question, there's work to do.

P
M

It's interesting you bring up skin. Our differing practices coalesce around what I refer to as 'permeable membranes'. There are different levels of permeability between the notion of Self and Others. There's an interplay of the permeable along these different degrees that we each use. I, for one, didn't always think being an artist was a profession available to me. As that came more into view, I had to consider how to protect myself and my work without closing myself off from everything else. There's a misconception that art exists in a bubble separate from the world, which annoys me. Do these notions of permeability manifest in your deployment of the vocabulary of illness – leakage, contamination, retention, rejection?

B
P

It's really the heart of my work. Truly, this question of permeability obsesses me. When you're lying prone in a hospital bed and the consultant makes the rounds, trailed by corps of medical students and interns, your interiority is penetrated by the sharp verticality of the medical establishment's power over you. You feel like your body doesn't belong to you anymore. It becomes a colonised, public space, like the hospital itself. There are depersonalising strategies at play, piercing you. Gestures can be penetrative in the clinical environment; needles literally pierce your body.

What interests me are the power structures – medical, social – that impact all bodies, not just ailing ones. It becomes a question of our capacity to determine the proverbial pores of our skin. If illness can diffuse outside of itself, can we produce alternative images of illness? Alternative discourses that are a little different, that deviate from the normative majority

Susan Sontag describes? She speaks of metaphors of illness.[2] It's those norms that invalidate those who are ill. There should exist a possibility to not simply be penetrated by society, but also flourish in the compost. I'm not saying illness is cool. I don't want to hide the detestable parts of these phenomena. But maybe it's more than *just* horrible? Maybe ill individuals don't have to be condemned to serve as sails, blowing in the direction of ableist, productivity-driven values.

P
M

I find that moving. I'm reminded of queer theory where a game of inversion volleys between the penetrated body and the penetrating body. In effect, all the violence that might be implied in underpinning these relations can also serve as a macro lesson in deconstructing, undoing, and collapsing those same interactions, not in a strictly utopian sense but by laying bare their difficulties and problematics, and the concrete realities of that violence. I see that a lot in your work. There's a utopian perspective that makes peace with its own impossibilities. I keep coming back to the notion of the membrane in your fabrics, for instance. There's a nuance that your chosen materials are charged with: they are nearly opaque but not entirely transparent. I find how your conceptions embrace that drift both pleasing and interesting. You spoke of Susan Sontag, and I know there are other figures, phantoms practically, that encircle the work. You speak often of Derek Jarman (1942–1994) and Monique Wittig (1935–2003). Are there others who serve as your companions?

B
P

Yes, there's a whole family. The Brazilian Baroque sculptor Aleijadinho (1738–1814) is a very important artist for me in terms of crip proto-history because of the singular manner in which he depicted bodies. I relate it to the way Jarman's book *Chroma* (1994) captured the depth of his memories as spatial explorations. Aleijadinho had a progressive illness that meant he lost his limbs over time, and so he made devices to allow himself to continue sculpting. He took an interest in alternative bodies, those which were not otherwise represented. Aleijadinho is someone who is on my wall.

Another 'artist' who interests me a lot is Margarete Steiff (1847–1909), the inventor of the toy stuffed animal. She had an illness from the time she was very little. She lost the use of one arm, and later her mobility was restricted to a wheelchair. She didn't have an occupation per se, but she did sew, which led to her making cuddly animals. The first form was a small elephant, sold on market stalls as a pincushion. Hers are forms that help us feel less afraid in the darkness. I started making stuffed animals, primarily bats. They allow me to give form to illness. Steiff, in her process, made a great number of memorial stuffed animals, for instance black bears to commemorate the sinking of the *Titanic*, marking collective grief. I find that so interesting. The presence and quality of their eyes was important. A few years later, a couturier in New York invented the 'teddy bear' and stole her thunder entirely. I'm struck by the fact that twenty years prior, a woman did it first, starting from a place of illness. In that compost, you find the power of coming up from under, of transgressing that membrane. So these are artists who are very present for me in my practice and for other reasons.

P
M

Another recurring apparition in your work is the bat, Monique.

B
P

Yes, Monique! I baptise my little bats 'Monique' for many reasons, especially in relation to two people, Monique Wittig and Roxanne Maillet. Wittig wrote *The Lesbian Body* (1973). The way she writes about the body sensualises fragmented bodies, and in turn, invalid bodies. I have an affinity with the nonbinary – in textures, in time, in the depth of things. Her book was a complete illumination! I like the notion of a collective body, where there's the possibility of sharing an intimacy, whether fragmented or singular.

Another biographical element from my life came during my childhood hospitalisation in a haematology centre. Several children requiring blood transfusions at that time were given HIV-contaminated blood. My body became more political from that moment onwards, because I was exposed to a virus that was fatal to most of the children. I was one of two children in my hospital to be exposed and survive. I felt compelled to do something after that. The idea of survival is something else. My body became collective at a very young age, which gave me, more than intimacy, a sense of collective interiority.

There are also the T-shirts of artist Roxanne Maillet, where she took the Nike swoosh and added the prefix 'Mo'. I found it subtle, and I profoundly connected with this provocation of 'MoNike'. I wanted to bestow a name that was a little bit generic, not a singularity. There's also a game to be played in that there is no linguistic norm with the spelling of Moneek, or Moneak. Sometimes I end it with -ck, at other times -que. It can have a 'k' or 'y' in it, or 'ea'. There's no one correct spelling.

P
M

To go back to this notion of a body that becomes collective, I remember exactly where I was – in the car – when I first heard the news on the radio about the contaminated blood, because we are roughly the same generation. It really impacted the collective imagination of my peers. It was a political moment in France that lodged itself in the public consciousness on the order of not just wariness about sickness or HIV/AIDS, but the fallibility of health care. Medicine wasn't as safe and regulated as we wanted to believe. In the wake of all of this, how do you find the means for your artistic practice to coexist with your illness in an arts industry that validates high productivity and doesn't necessarily have much interest in accommodating different needs and paces?

B
P

That's equally part of work, in fact. I give workshops with students who are still in art school. The curators I work with, the art foundations and the institutions themselves are brought into my waiting room, or at least I try to transform the exhibition space into my recovery room, to transpose my hospital bed into the gallery. I'm more a patient than an exhibiting artist. I also have to interact with the wider teams. I have a protocol that I have been putting into place for a while now when working with teams, where I ask for their used bars of bath or shower soap. They are intimate portraits that I turn into collective photos by shooting the bars of soap together. I offer this image back to the team as a class photo.

Sometimes the portraits are shown in situ. It's interesting that this corporeal intimacy has a visible expression. It speaks of consent, of bodies that are absent. 'Think clean' or 'Think dirty.' It's also about the composition of soap itself: caustic soda and oil that go through an irreversible reaction when the two combine at just the right temperature, suddenly becoming a caress that no longer exists once it's served its purpose. The disappearance is inherent, yet here are sensual, salaried bodies. There are lots of ways to invest my time and energy.

Time and productivity are linked in my practice, but not in the usual way. Productivist timelines are completely linear, but I invest 'my time', which is completely circular. There's no beginning and no end. My temporality is illness. Being invited to develop a commission, which for me is inextricably linked to my illness, means I have to bring the temporality of illness back into the circuit of productivity. Producing an exhibition in a short time span isn't necessarily possible for me, or at a minimum, it requires other collaborators to be brought in. All these questions become budget lines and you have to, in some ways, predict the unpredictable. Maybe on the day of the opening I'm not well enough to get myself there. A taxi therefore becomes not so much a luxury as a necessity. We might not have to send for an ambulance – though that has been the case – but my real, practical needs do have to be factored in from the start. So, the work could be called 'activist' in the sense that one has to start with accounting for those necessary line items. There's a mediation and a nonviolent communication that re-establishes the institutional framework. Accept / expect the unexpected, and don't assume an ableist capacity for response times.

P
M

This resonates. Coming back to permeability and the space of welcome, collectivity or intimacy, we come of course to the question of the invitation. An invitation resonates strongly with notions of consent and shared responsibility. I'm struck by – and I know this is true for many arts workers – the many criteria that can marginalise us, that leave us tasked with doing the work that the institution should be responsible for delivering. So, it's true, I've found it useful to implement certain strategies so that I don't wind up depleted by the demands the institution might make of me.

B
P

We need only to consider Felix Gonzalez-Torres (1957–1996) to know we aren't all alone in this adopting of strategies so as not to illustrate the illness but to navigate as an internal pathogen would. There are different positions, different stances to take. David Wojnarowicz (1954–1992) took the external route, for instance standing on the street corner.[3] Gonzalez-Torres found a way to enter the institution without altering his discourse. I understand entirely where you are coming from, not wanting your essence to be aspirated. You used a term I find interesting: 'implemented'.

P
M

I transliterated it from English!

B
P

I think it's a good term. What does it mean?

P
M

To implement is similar to integrating, to bring in methods and strategies that protect me. I speak about it a lot with art students and young artists. Which is why I brought it up with you. When art has such intrinsic links with our lives, with who we are – in my case this is particularly true with performance, maybe less so with my installations or designs when my body isn't physically present – I have to ask myself: What do I give? What do I hold back? They are questions of survival. What can you allow yourself to give? These are delicate questions because of the expectations around certain artists. And when I say 'certain artists' I mean those of us who aren't necessarily part of the status quo. How can we *not* be devoured by institutional mechanisms designed to destroy us?

B
P

I want to come back to the idea of consent. With Monyk, you have to allow her in. In vampire lore, vampires must be invited in via a doorway or a window. She can't enter unless invited. So as I think about needles (and many things) it equips me to answer the second part of the question. I have complete imagery of my body based on 3D scans made by doctors to prepare me for surgery. To give those images over to others so that they can play with my body – move it, cut it up, penetrate it – that becomes a reappropriation.

P
M

I see something in that demonised European folklore, the perception of malevolent beings. I've been thinking about the notion of the vampire in the entirely different research context of roller-rink culture on the South Side of Chicago. For a predominantly Black community, poor and socially disenfranchised, roller skating is a practice for survival. I began to think of the vampire as an undead body, always in survival mode. Those links between blackness and perseverance, to eking out a life, but not necessarily evil.

B
P

I exist in a circular time frame because I am outside of the binary, the polarities of life and death. I came out of that demarcation very early on, at such a tender age, having been born with meningitis. Illness is the living incarnation of death. Society gives us these costumes, holding us up against the paragons of efficiency and productivity. What I sense in your roller-skaters analogy makes me think of an artist friend of mine who set off on a skateboard, laden with heavy bags like he was setting sail on a barge. There was a sensuality in his movements, caressing public space in a way that reminded me of how we caress our phones when scrolling. Something in my work approaches that state; it's so much about survival that it ceases being *just* about survival. You're making love to surviving. It's carnal. When bodies are desexualised, made invisible, a radical softness comes into it. There's a sensuality in the tools and materials I select. The fabrics. The needles I use, which can also be found in various forms of alternative healing practices, but also in kink. These are all ways to reconnect with one's interiority and transform sickness to get closer to one's sexuality, something sensual. Alternate explorations of sexuality that aren't normative and are often invalidated have the potential to enrich all sexualities and expand the norms. Thinking about this is like travelling without moving. It's been such a long time since I went skating! Maybe I'll get my roller skates back on one day.

P
M

Yes, there's something about not going against things, making do with and giving

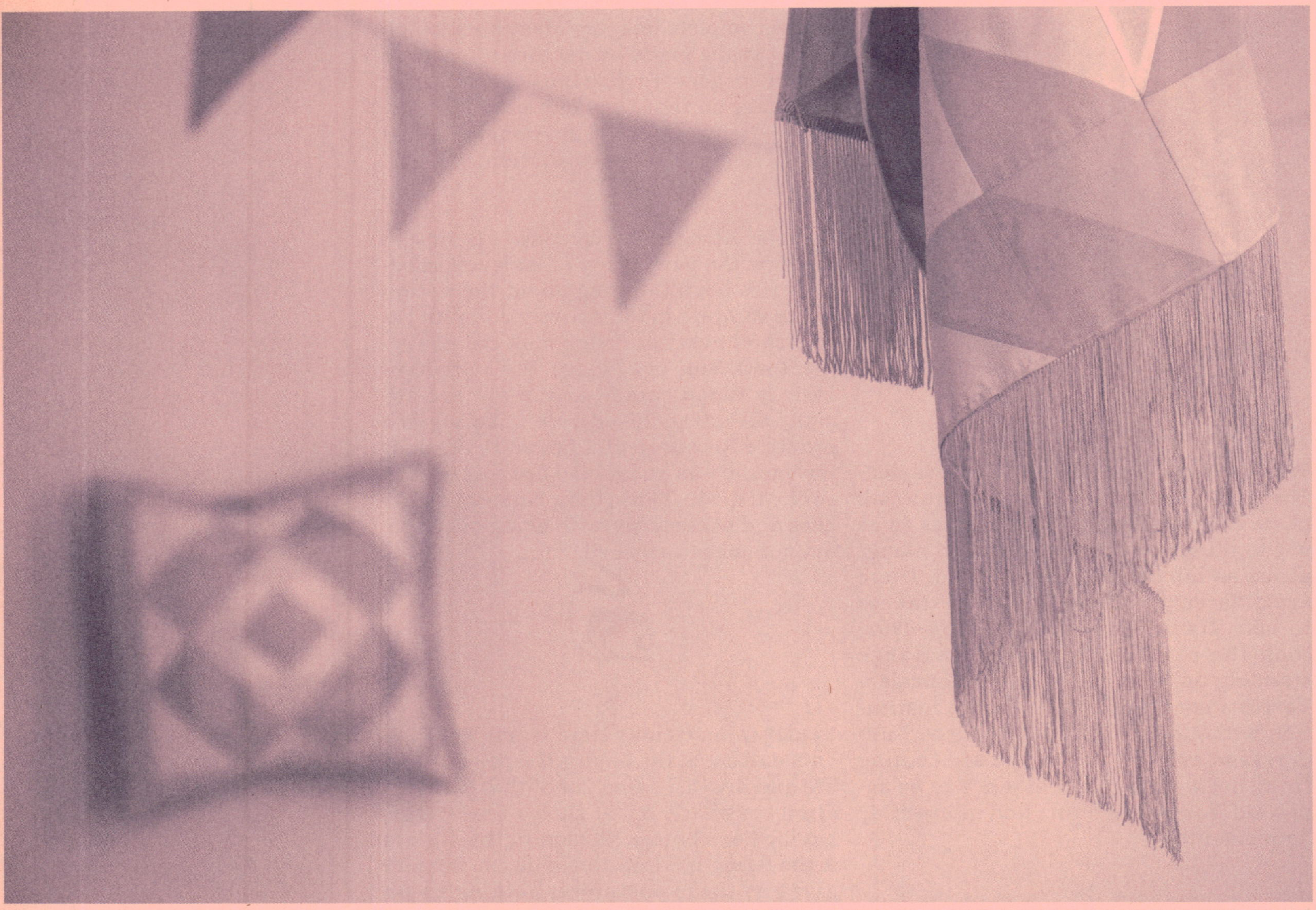

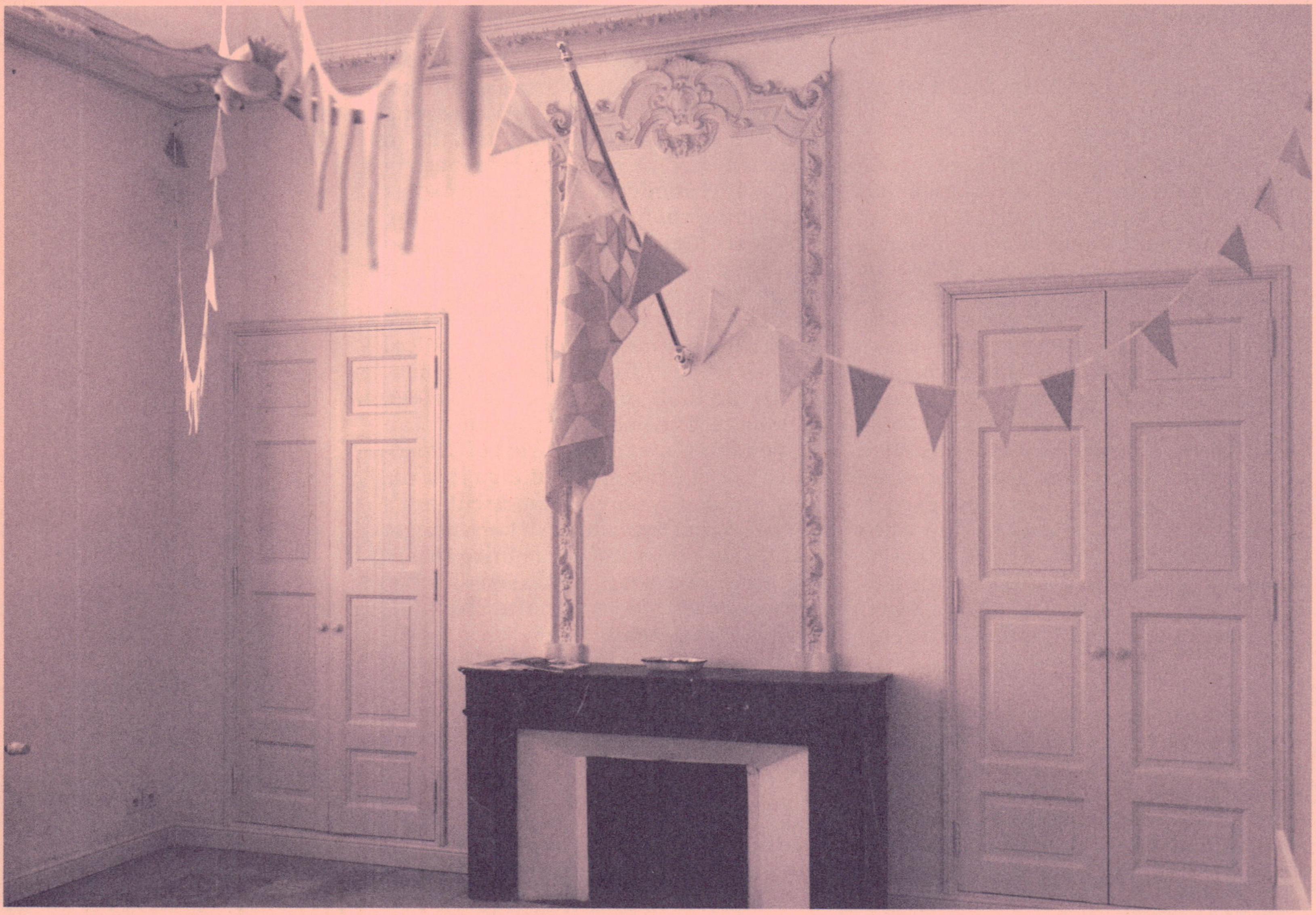

oneself to gravity. It's not even subversive. It's about pleasure and yielding to it. Let's talk now about your Chisenhale Gallery commission, your first solo exhibition in the UK.

B
P

Well, a while ago Olivia Aherne, Zoé Whitley, and I started to envision this project. It's been a very long process, born in the space, in an experiential way. I was in the gallery with Olivia, the exhibition's curator, and at a certain moment I started to slide, blob-like, onto the ground. I became a puddle. The room at the time was sort of draped in concrete thanks to Nikita Gale's *In a Dream You Climb the Stairs* (2022), and at a certain magic hour in the late afternoon, the sun reflected off the canal through the windows and onto the gallery walls. Olivia slid and joined me on the floor, where we continued our intellectual conversation between artist and curator. My illness made its presence known, and diffused itself in the space. We achieved a moment of grace and total empathy. That's my true medium: empathy. I've realised that the people who interest me most have it. The expression of empathy is also linked to neurodivergence and needs to be redefined in terms beyond heteronormative sentiment. I try to recognise the power of emotional interconnectedness. The incidence of my illness rearing its head suddenly, bringing me to the ground, happened within the beauty of that room, the light playing on the walls. What happened became the basis for our thinking of travelling through illness, approaching the psychedelic – the labyrinth, the kaleidoscope.

For the commission, I'm creating a huge patchwork from recycled medical gowns and bedding. Scaled to fit the gallery architecture, it becomes a tablecloth, suspended so that we can get underneath – a gesture that signals the power of what lies beneath, rather than what comes from above. It's not rigid, it submits to gravity. There's a political dimension to the hanging mechanism. This cloth will be pitched from a post which is actually a table leg. This table leg is topped by a red-domed pincushion of the type worn on the wrist when sewing, as when making little stuffed animals or creatures. At the same time, it's catheter-like. It's so important to me, the catheter. This oversized intimate item becomes outsized, reminiscent of spaces where a tablecloth can become a child's under-table den.

Olivia tracked down a textile waste processing plant near the gallery, called Coppermill, that recycles medical gowns and bedding. Once they are too stained for continued circulation in British hospitals, they arrive there to be treated and transformed: the fabric turns into cleaning rags, cloths, tea towels, even filler for boxing gloves! Some of the flat sheets, when they're beyond repair, are sent to local prison services and made into cot sheets and pillowcases. All of these reuses are equally interesting to me, knowing that a good portion of these textiles will be repurposed from former users who are deceased. I received a babygro full of black stains, which suggests the presence of iron and of the garment having undergone a sanitising process because it must have been covered in blood.

These are 'off-screen' occurrences that must be carefully managed, and I try to approach them with extreme gentleness. Some things are very hard to address in a gallery, which is where the childlike animism comes in: I draw on the walls with Crayola but the crayons were made with my own blood, referring to what attempted to stay hidden in the contaminated-blood scandal. Impure blood is now on open display on the walls, just like I also display my medical scans. These things could weigh me down if I kept them hidden away. But out in the open they take on sociability, making the gallery space a body, a theatre for sociability.

P
M

In relation to this exhibition, are there any particular encounters you dream of? Moments in the space you'd like to see?

B
P

It is about moments, for me. I want to see what happens when what we've produced can be shared as a collective experiment: what we're doing right now, you and me, or my work with the team, with craftspeople, with fabricators, it's all such a crucial part of the process. As with my textile works using decommissioned hospital linens, the imprint of each person who touched it previously remains. There's an emotional charge, an arduous charge, a laborious charge, a pleasurable charge, but also the joy, the pain, the suffering, all laden within the work's production. That's important: the ecology of each piece's own distinct energy. I don't project onto others because I exist in an ever-present sense of circular time. There's no rear-view mirror. I'm just in the present moment, in depth.

There's something childlike present in the commission too, in that wondrous animism of childhood. We find this in Moneeq: the presence of this little vampire embodying sickness in a palatable form that we are unafraid to look in the eye. It's a form that makes acceptance possible. There's the notion of the

p. 20, 23
Benoît Piéron, *Illness Shower* (2022). Installation views, Sultana Summer Set, Arles, 2022. Photo: Benoît Piéron. Courtesy of Galerie Sultana.

undead, obviously. There was also an indelible moment of encounter with the team that manifested around the large communal table in the gallery's studio space. All of us gathered around the sheaves of scoubidou (PVC string) I brought for crafting. I met most of the team throughout the day, making small things with those who wanted to. That approach of introducing myself through shared making became a useful sidestep to see things from different angles and new perspectives. For me, that's the root of the project.

Lighting games like the zoetrope, historic plays on optical motion and also girofar lights that vary in intensity are also part of the exhibition. In the climax of a film, these light often used on emergency vehicles symbolise the power of redemption for some characters and a more tragic outcome for others – it might be that all of a sudden, firefighters are arriving on the scene to save the hero, for example. That flashing light equally gets woven into the fabric of our fears. So there's this double meaning, as it can be a violent kind of light. Just think of cops using the stroboscopes on their flashlights to induce a disorienting kind of neurological terror.

Olivia and I are going to put little ombre hats on the lights, referencing the radical gentleness of the colours seen in nail art, as an urgent counterpoint to the violence. Like putting a silencer on a trumpet. It's a bit like my bat, something that enables us to look at another reality occurring beyond our range of experience. Like the quilt, the stains we don't want to see, usually hidden away in hospitals, get held up to the light. A transformation occurs. Something relaxing, hypnotic, and pleasurable that started off as something hard and difficult. It's like the moment when the Chisenhale Gallery team first invited me – the 'come in' to the vampire. I'm the little vampire in the institution.

P
M

It's the compost breaking down so that the ecosystem can thrive. The work lives before and beyond its initial moment of public reveal in the exhibition space.

B
P

Maybe we can think of it as a slumber party? Living with illness, is it possible to celebrate that fact, as one might a baby shower? With Olivia, it felt more like making preparations for a pyjama party. When you think about it, the little populace of the ill is a populace of pyjama wearers!

P
M

And one final, final question: What's the question you never get asked and would like to be asked?

B
P

I'm never asked: For whom do you create? I'm not quite sure who said it, but 'there's no poetry without death.' And it's a question I don't get asked directly: Who do I make art for?

P
M

Do you want to answer?

B
P

I have referenced it before, but it's for my best friend, who died of AIDS when I was little. We spent a lot of time together. His name was Jeremy. It's the name behind my patchwork. Patchwork is so often about memory, it's often political. Think of the NAMES Project AIDS Memorial Quilt or how patchwork is used in relation to the disappeared in Latin America.

P
M

A permanent homage. It's an interesting question for me, too: the mode and direction of address. There can be multiple intended addressees.

B
P

Of course. It's for all of them. Because once people are dead, that intended person becomes both very fixed but also vaporous, and they're easy to satisfy aesthetically!

This conversation took place between Piéron and Maheke over video call on Saturday 5 August 2023.

1 'We are compost, not posthuman; we inhabit the humusities, not the humanities. Philosophically and materially, I am a compostist, not a posthumanist.' Donna J. Haraway, *Staying with the Trouble: Making Kin in the Chthulucene* (Durham, NC: Duke University Press, 2016), 97.

2 Susan Sontag, *Illness as Metaphor* (London: Penguin, 1978).

3 As in David Wojnarowicz, *Untitled ('Friendly Cow' for Peter Hujar)*, 1982.

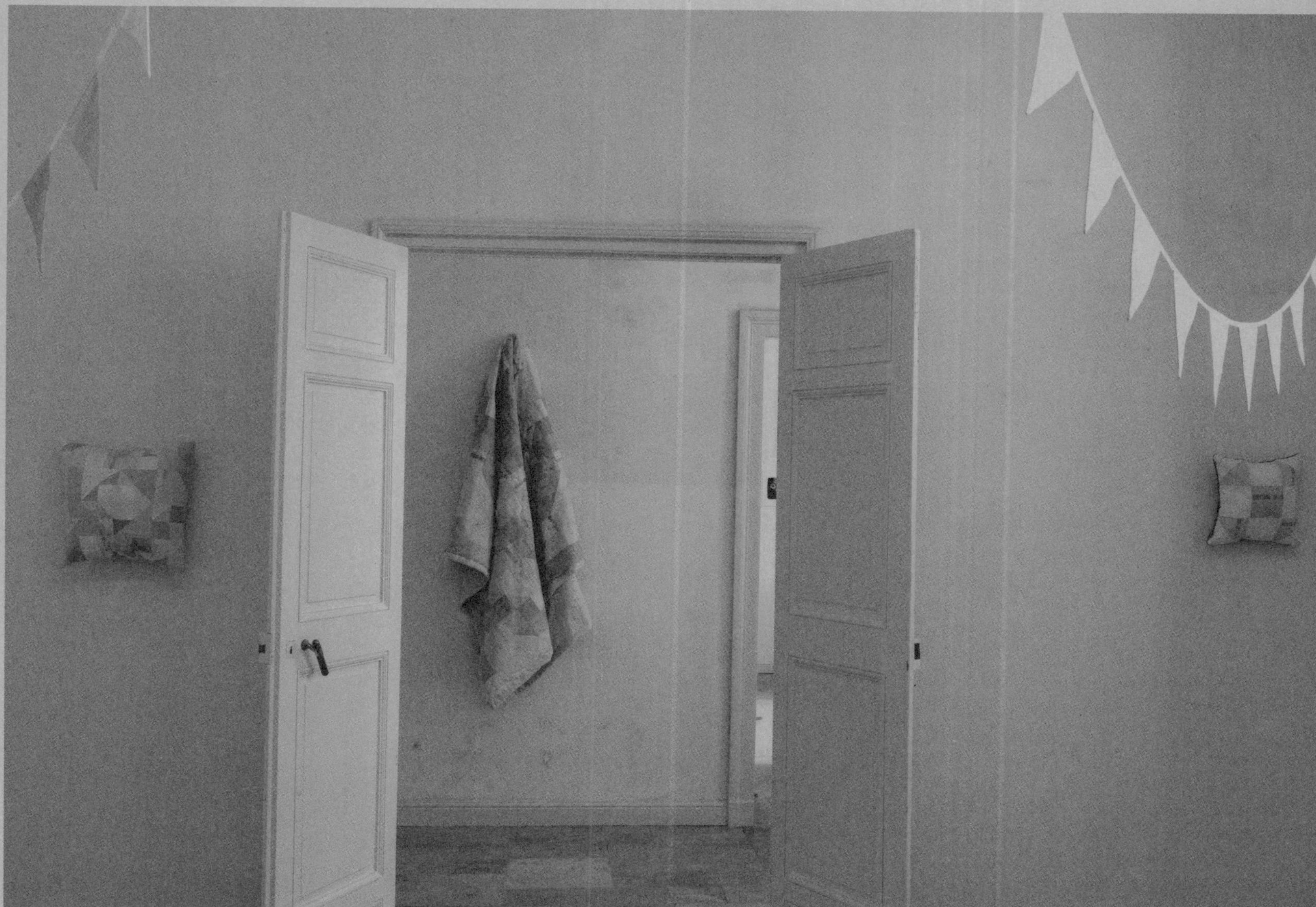

SLUMBER

P
A
R
T
Y

CHISENHALE
GALLERY

LONDON
2023

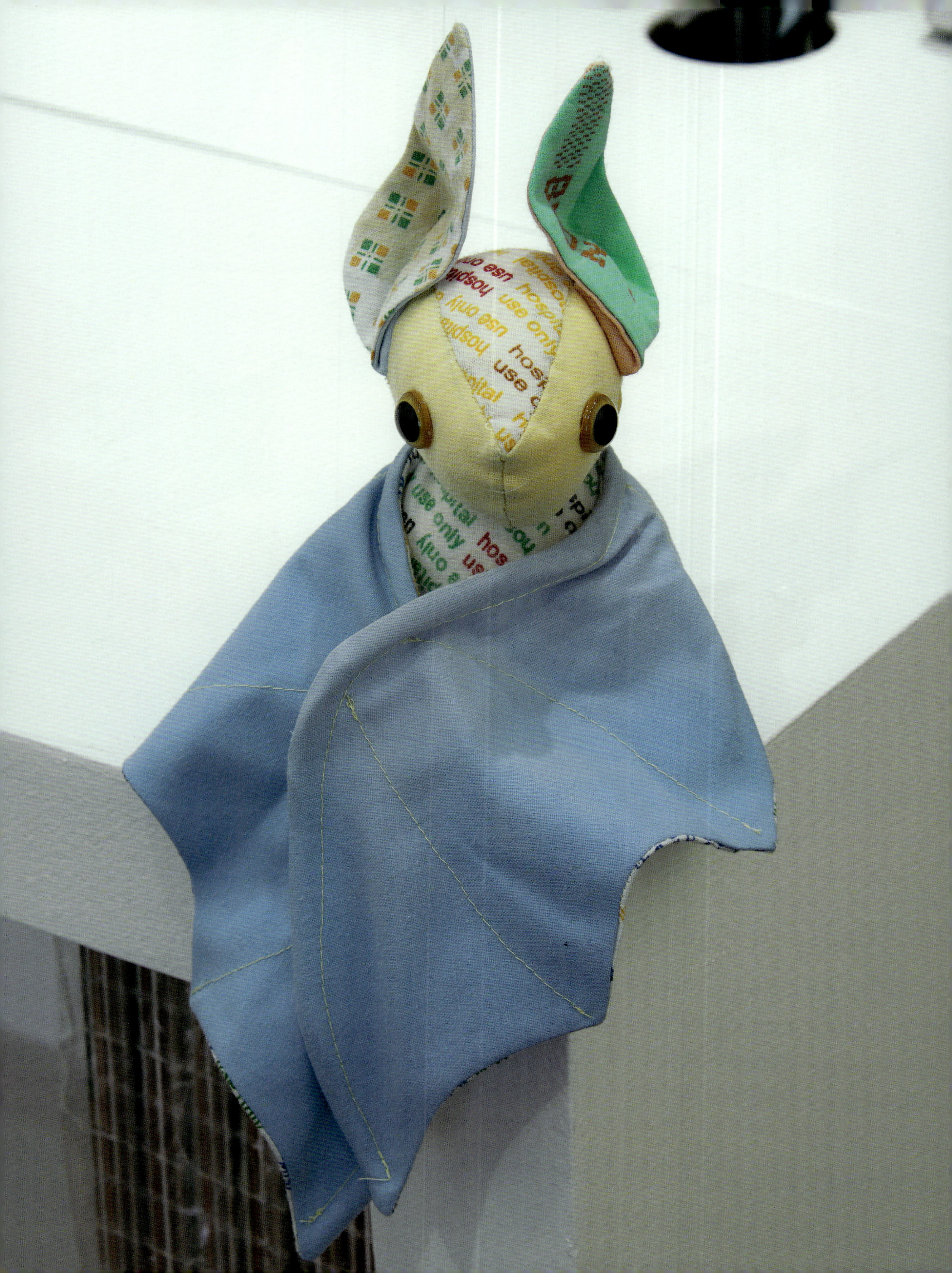

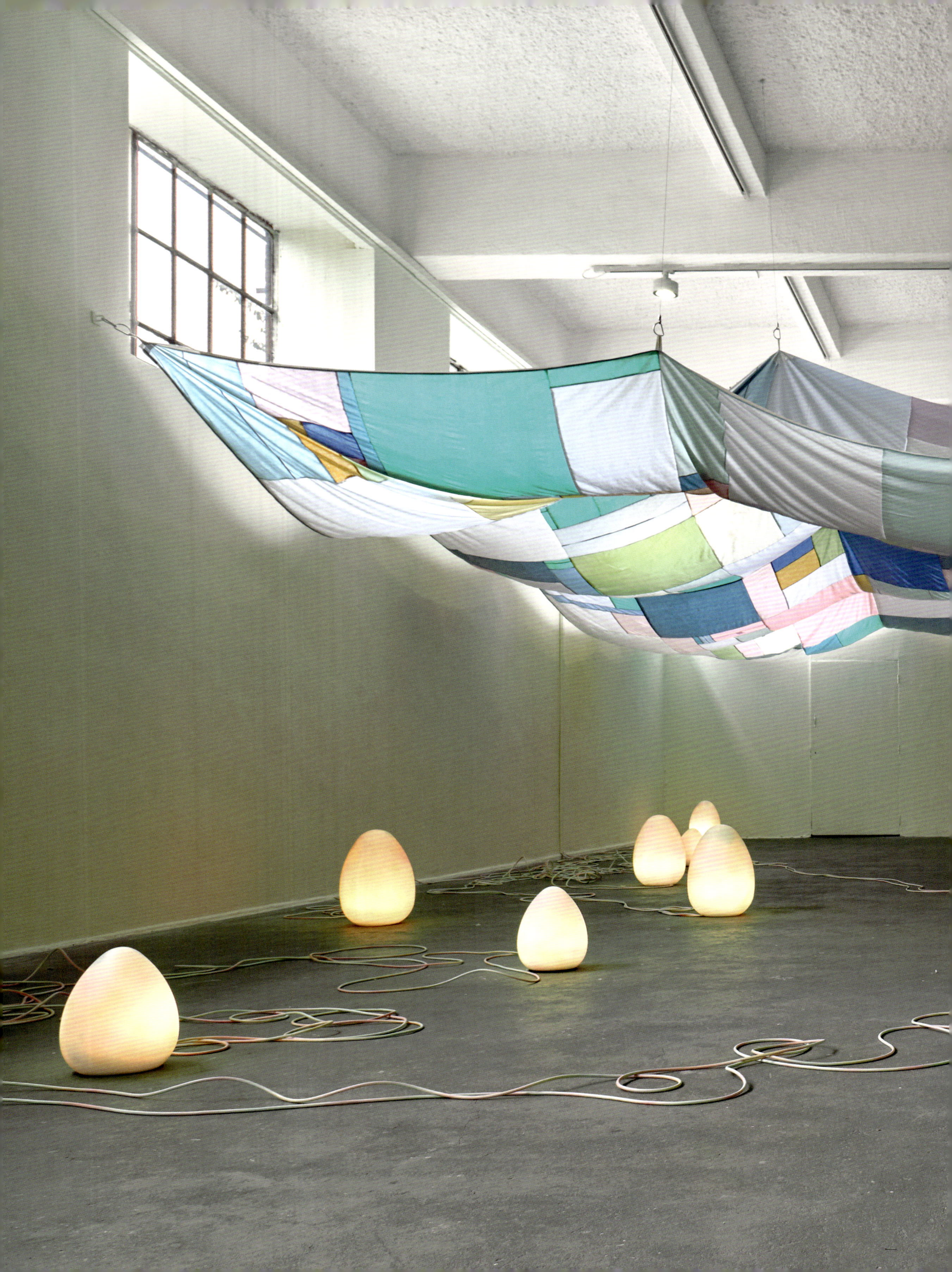

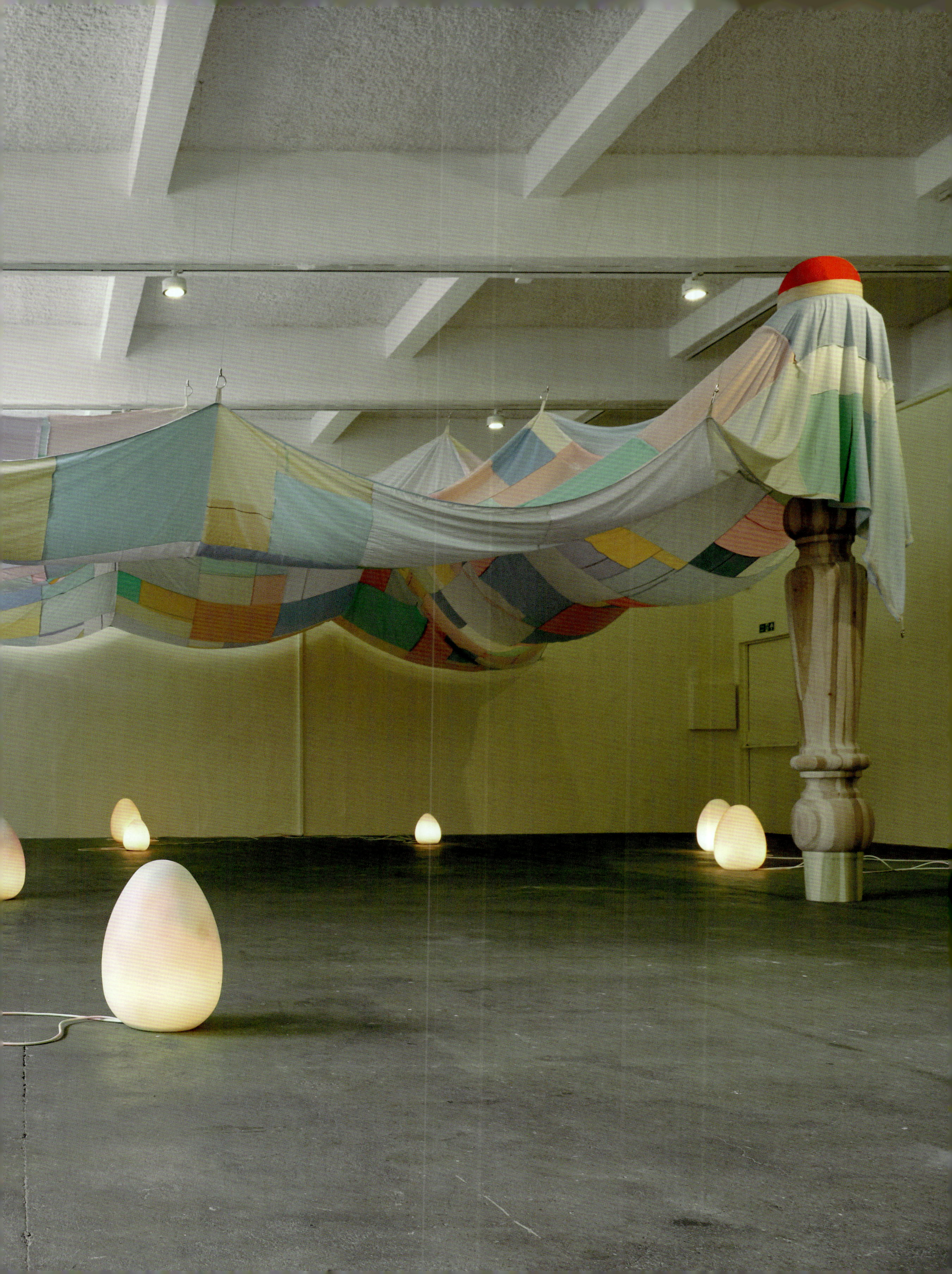

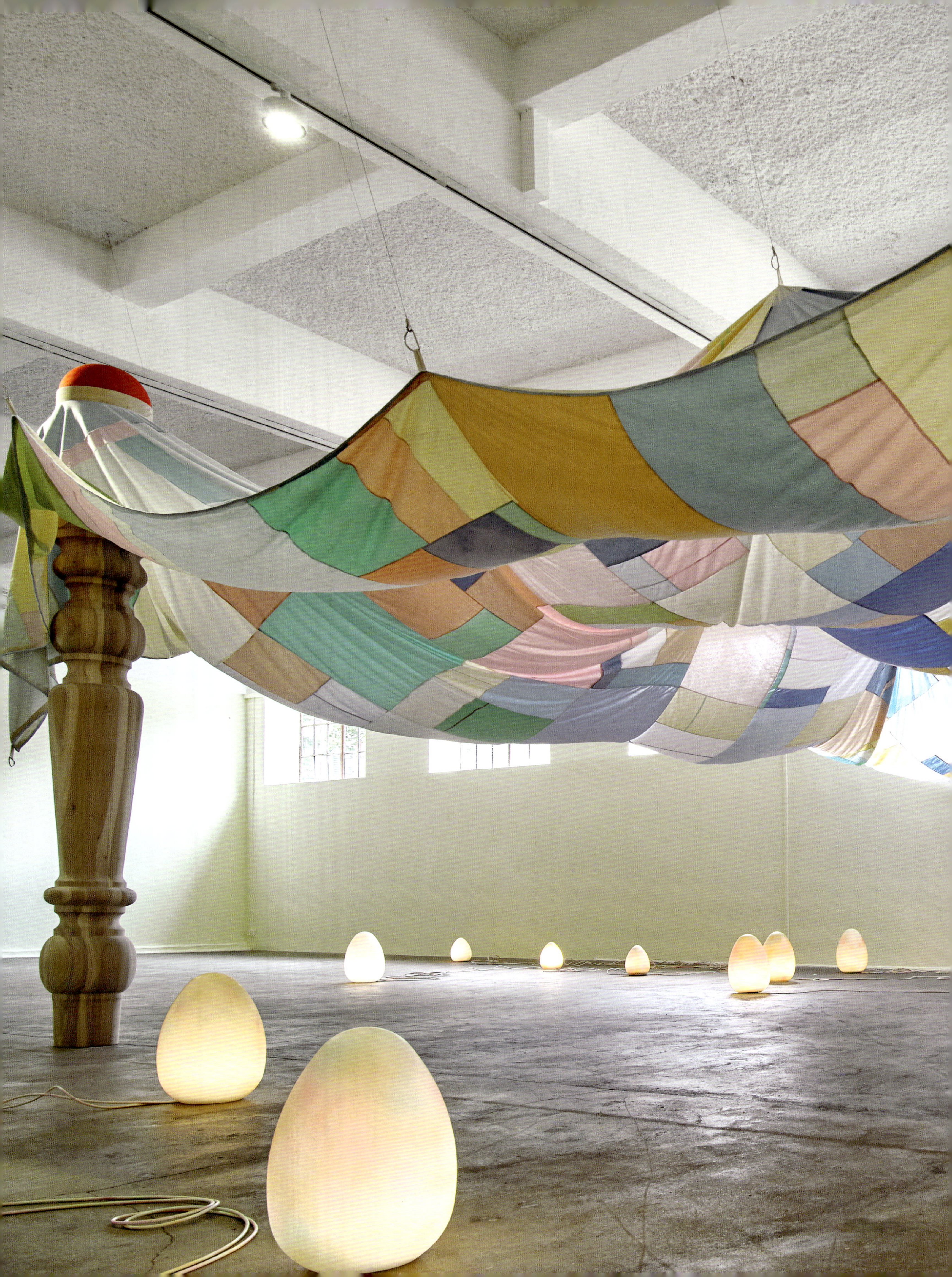

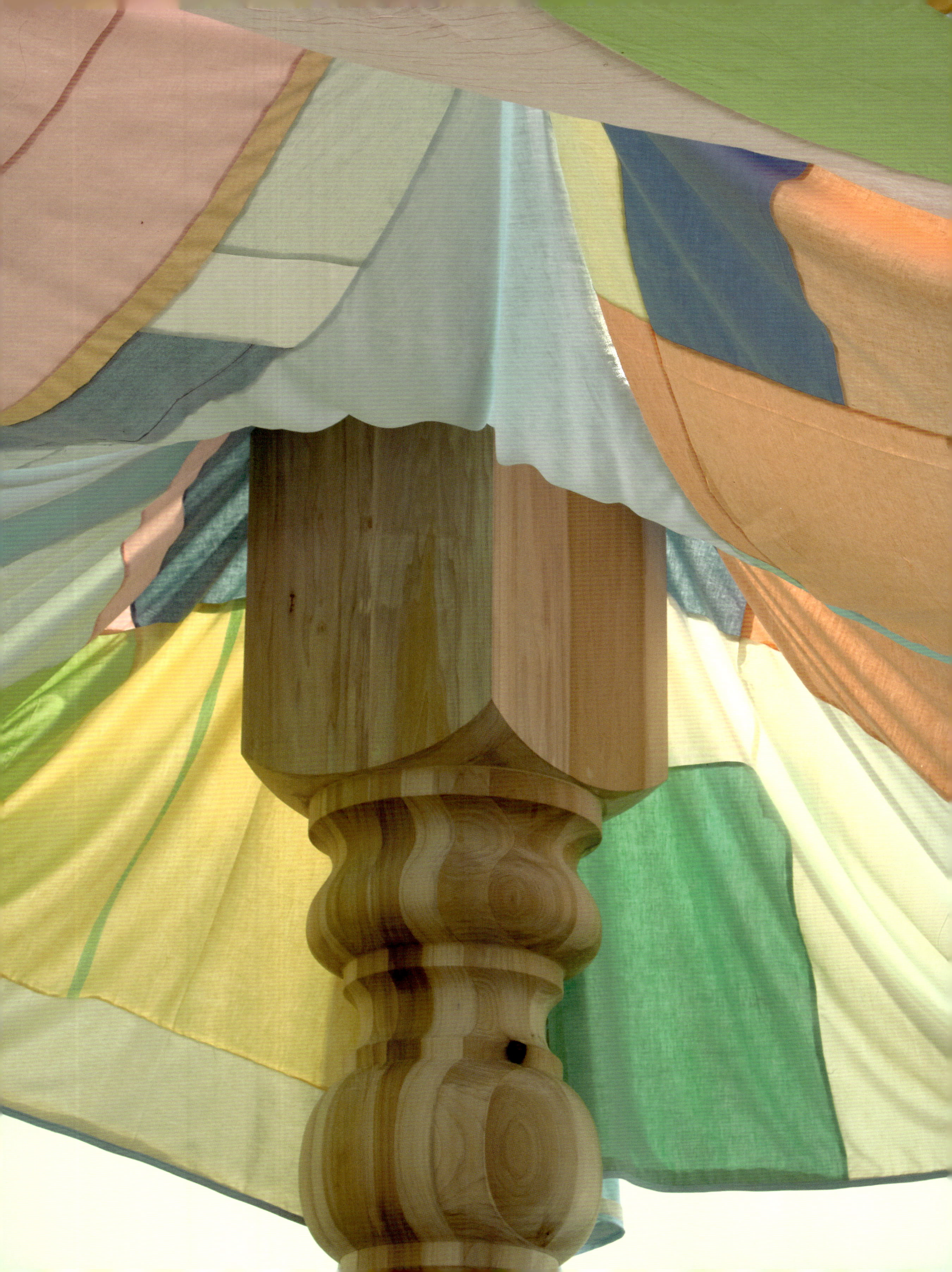

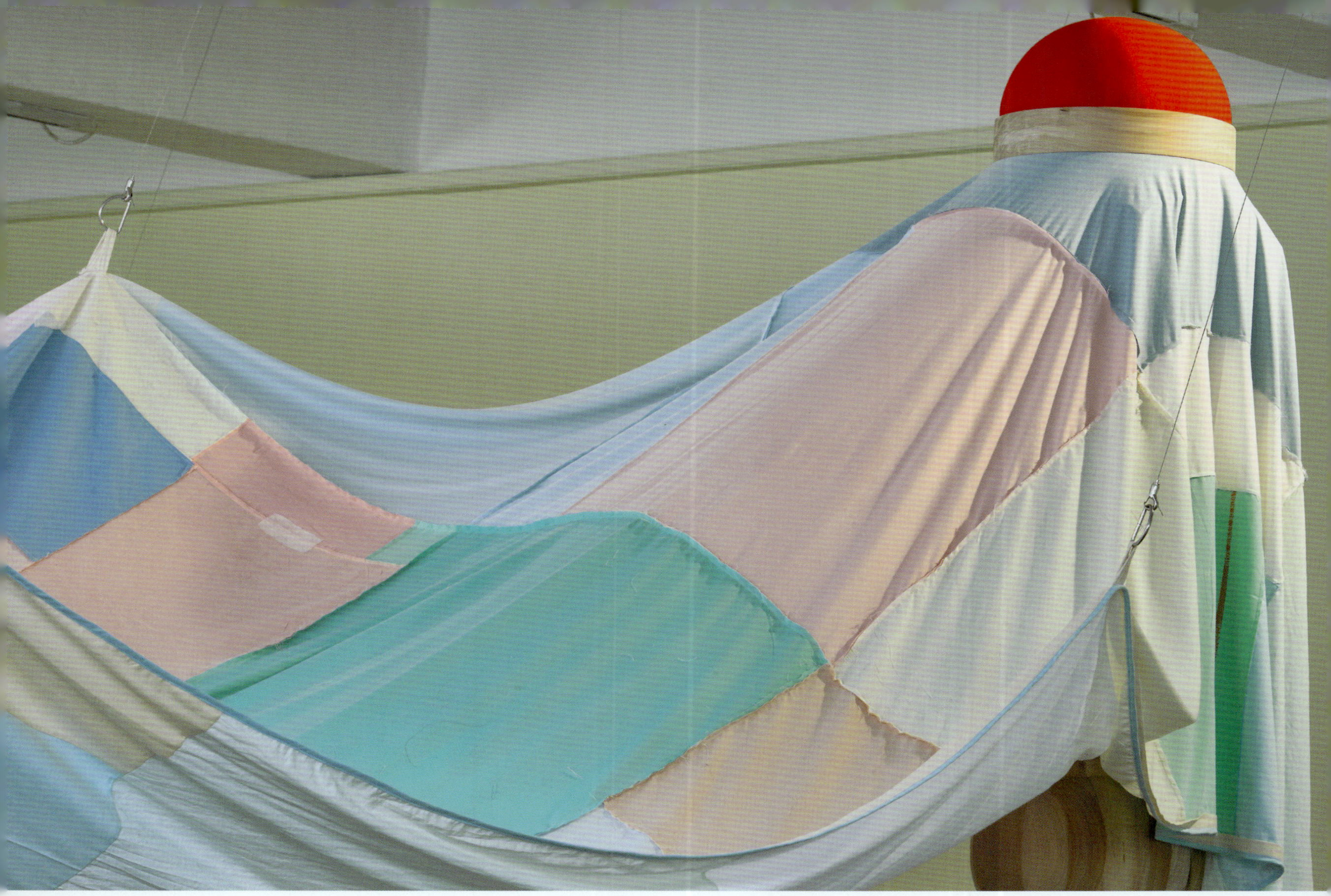

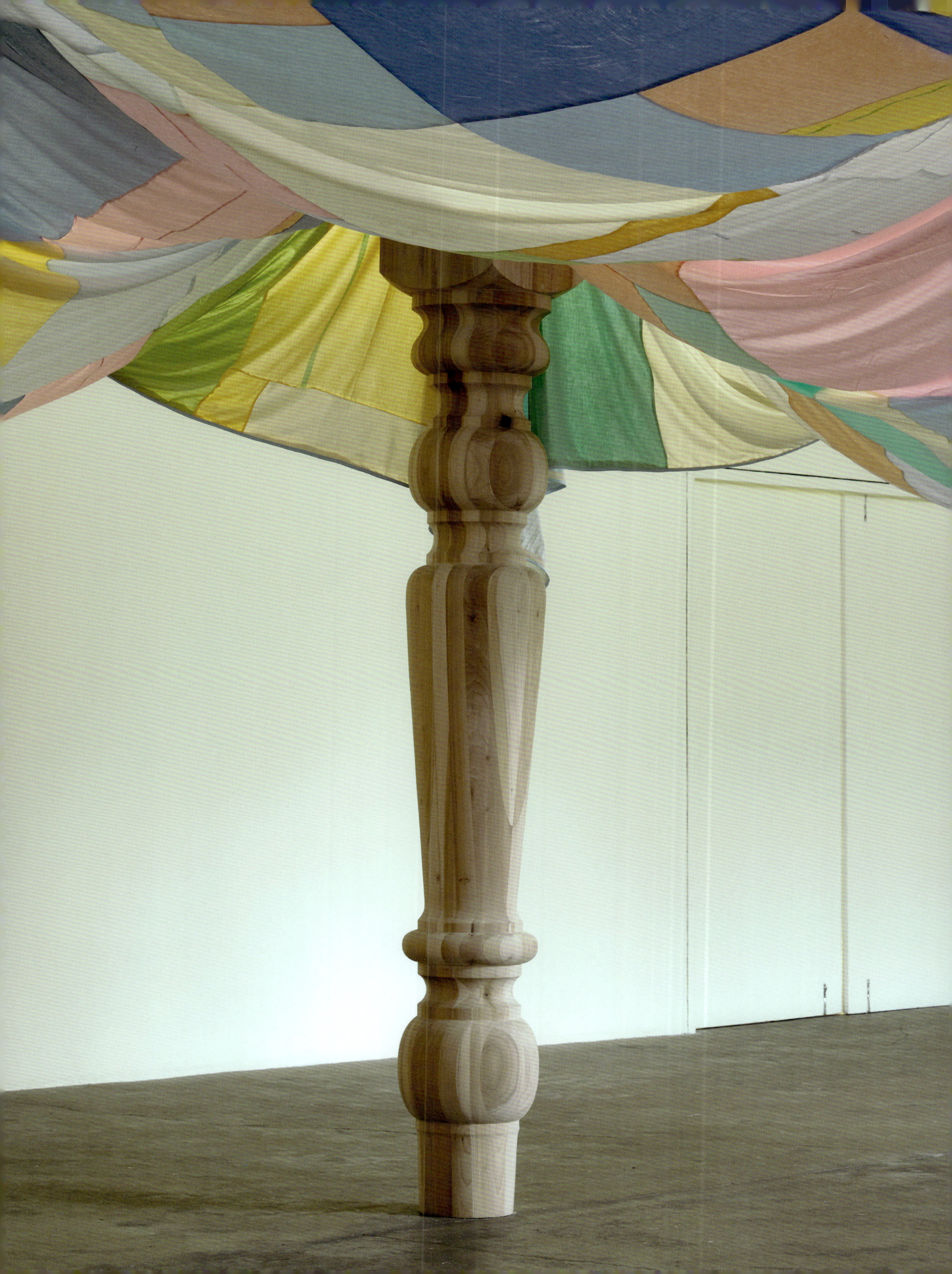

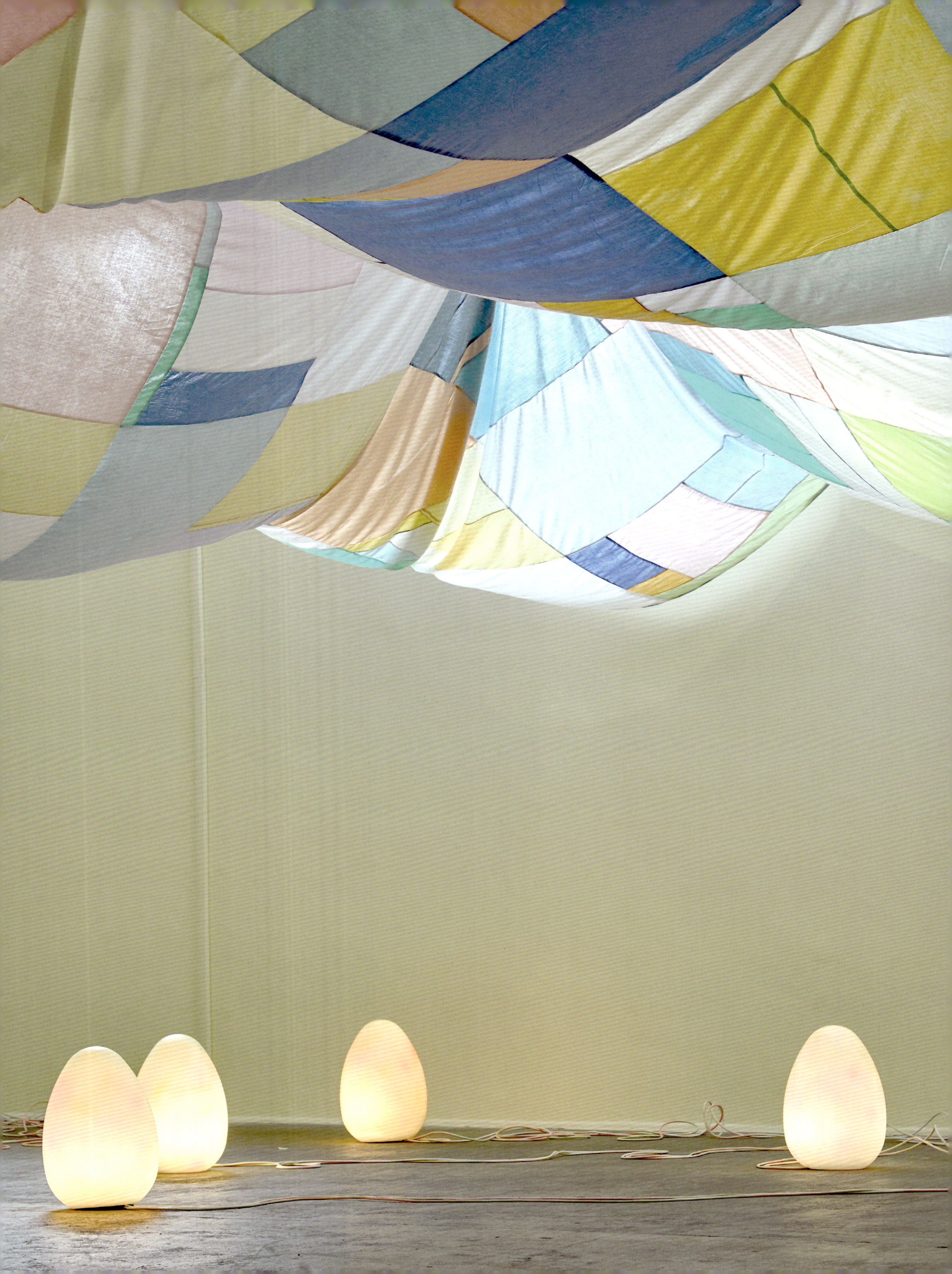

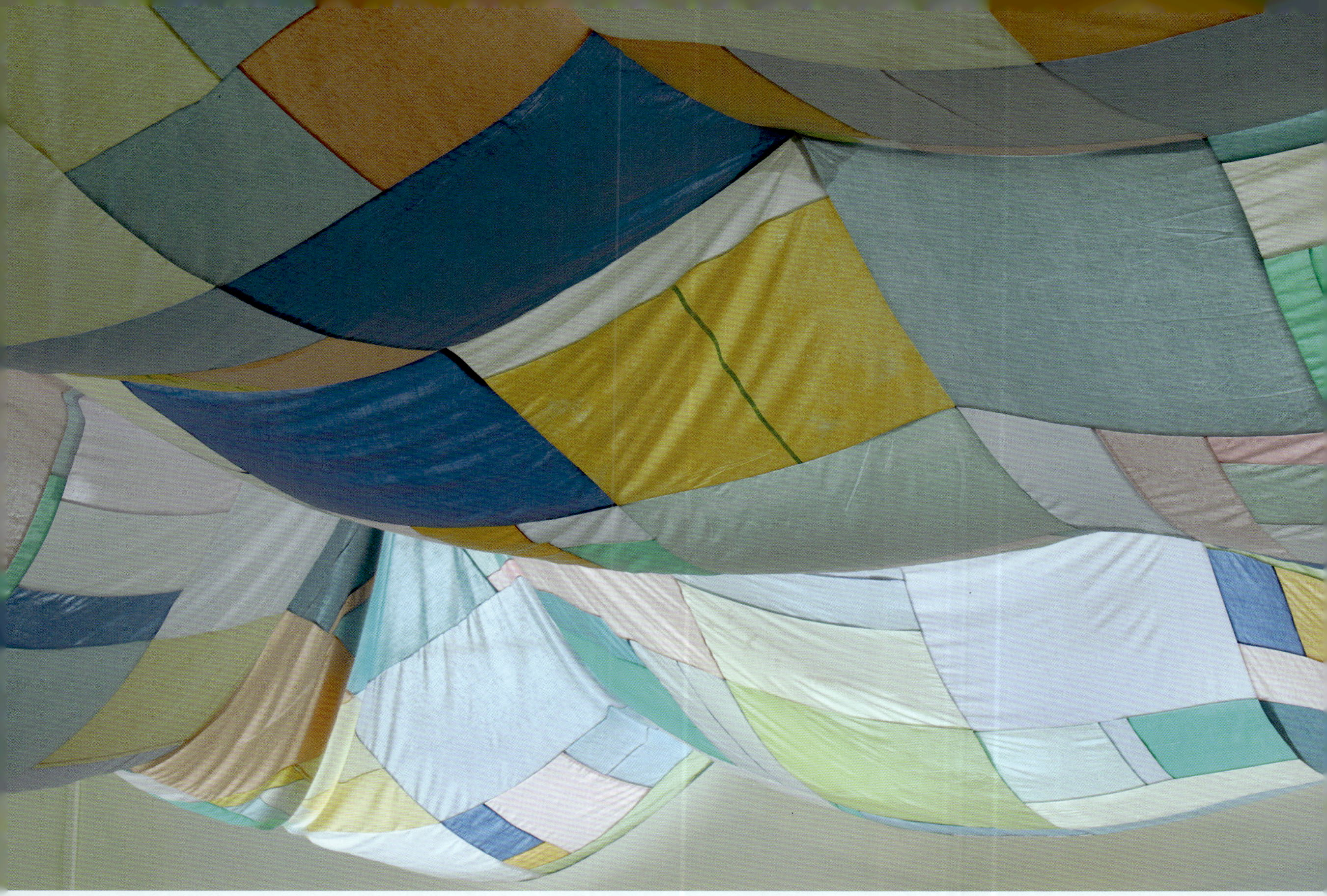

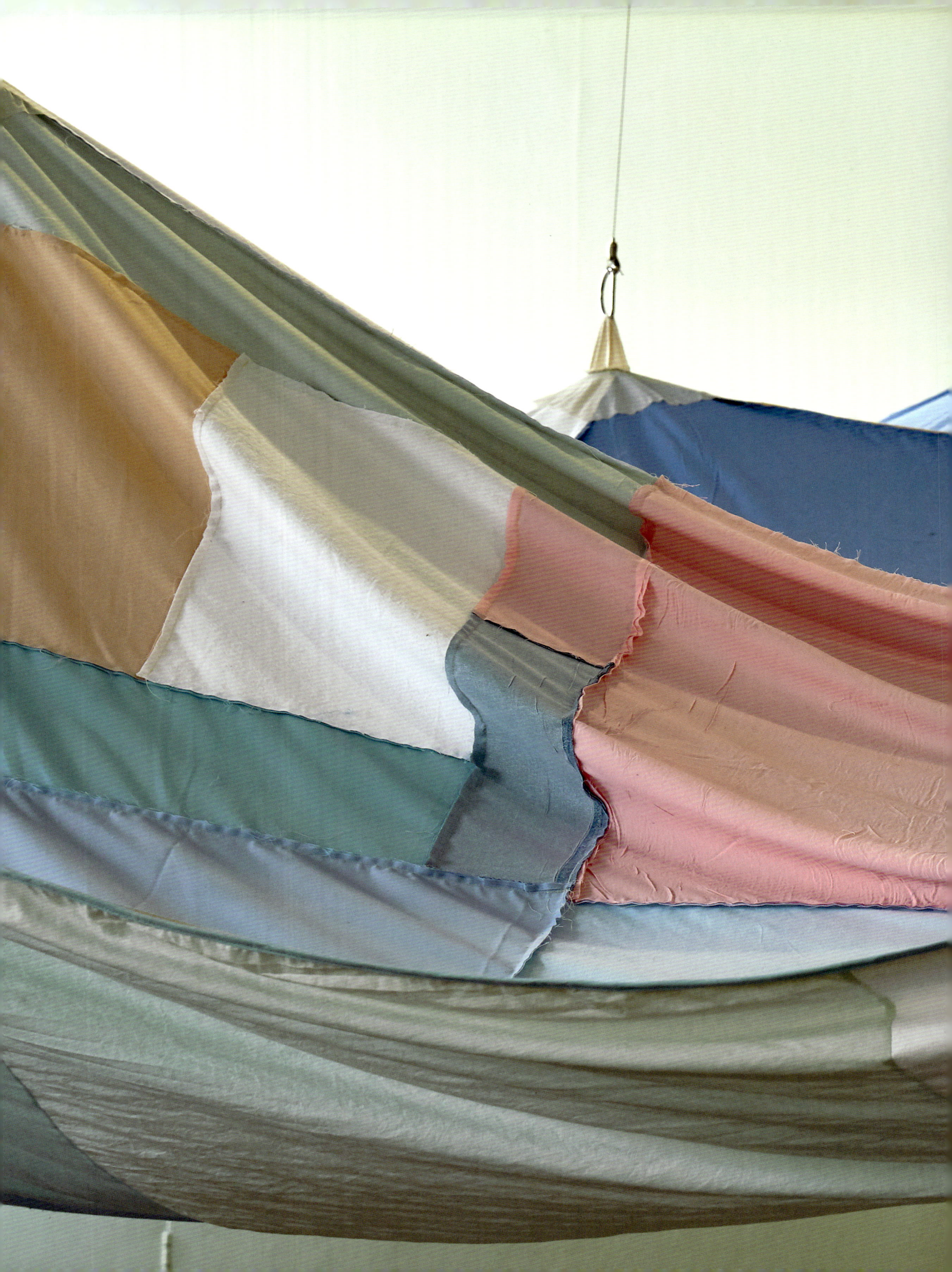

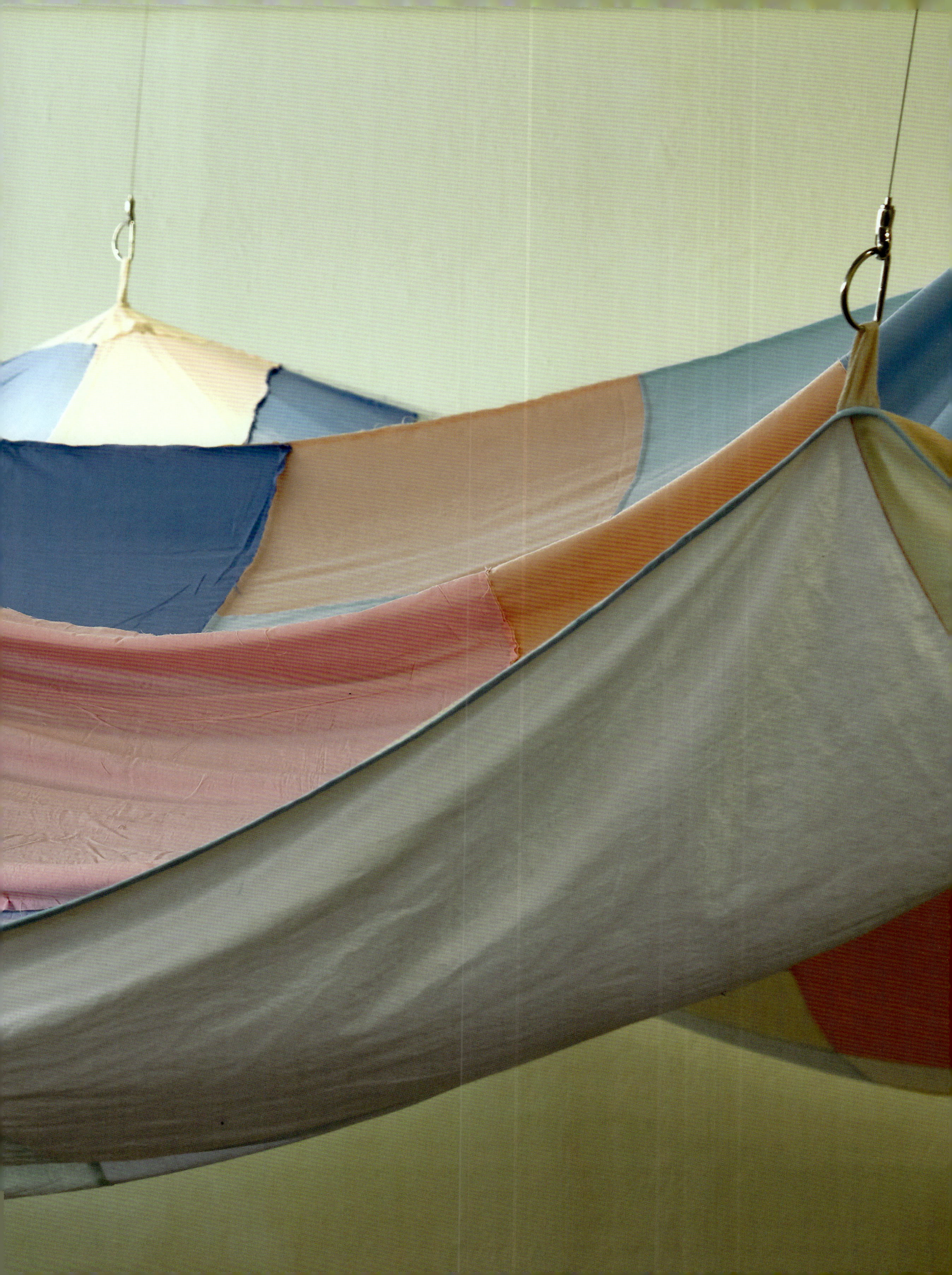

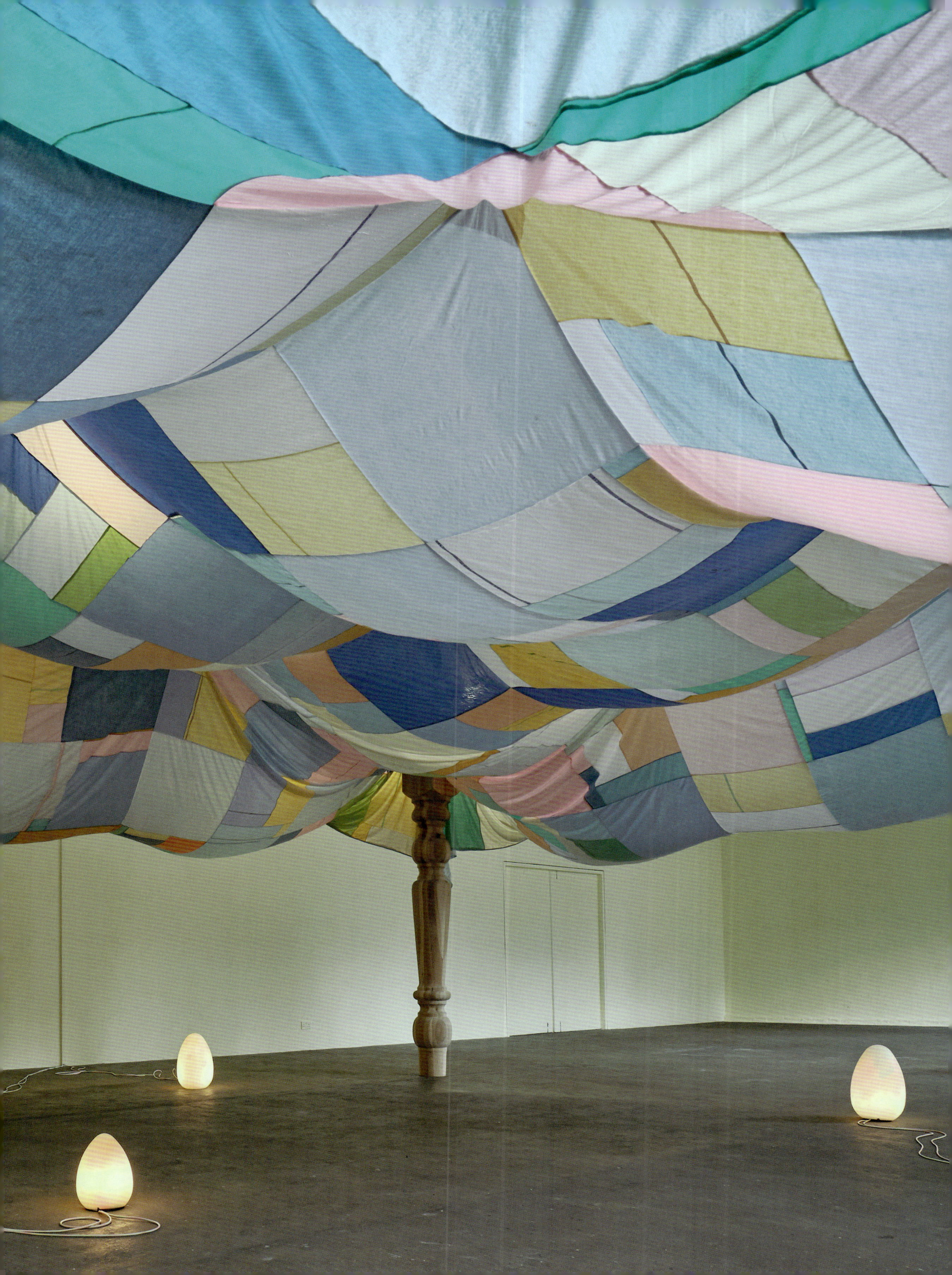

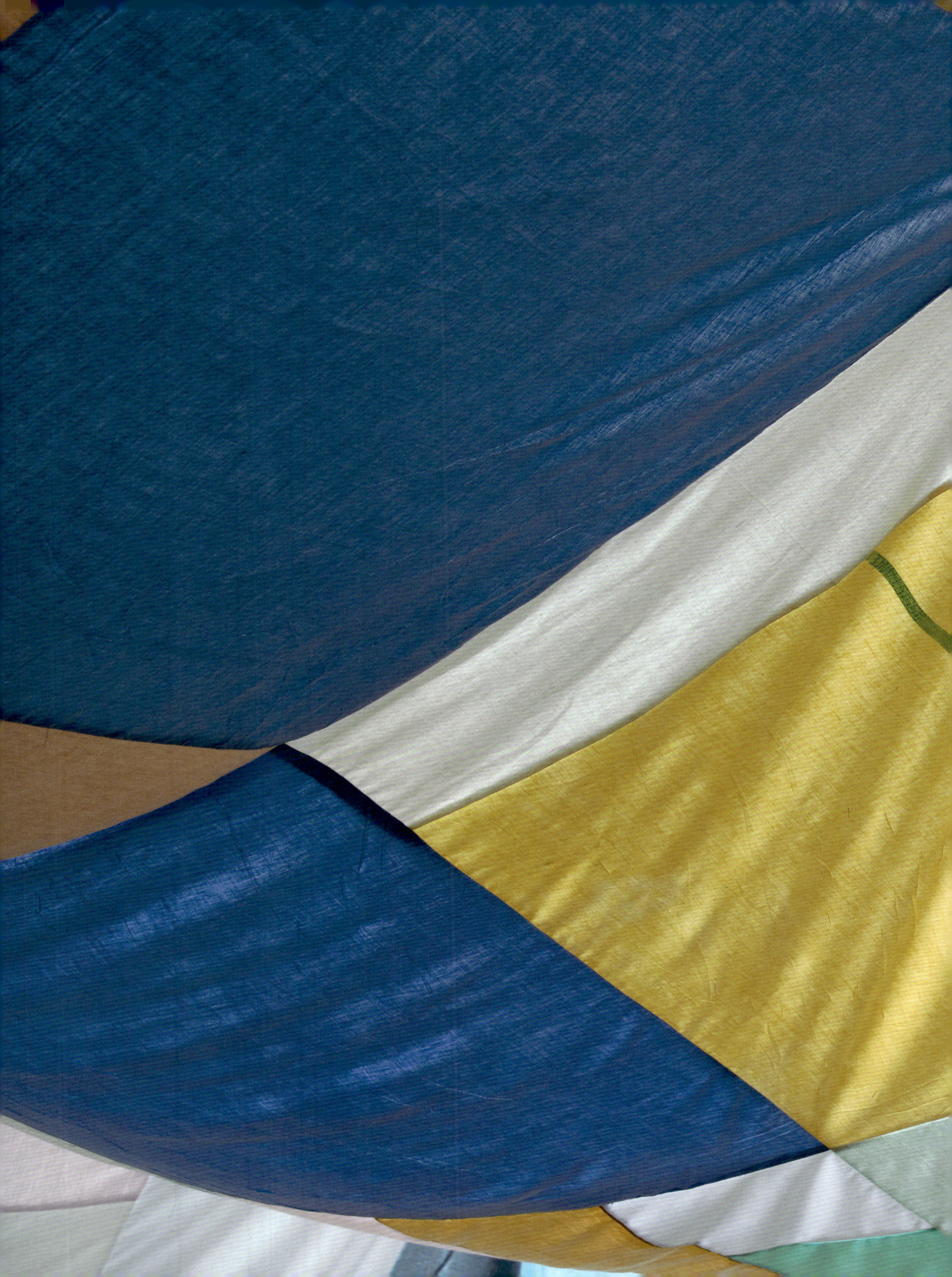

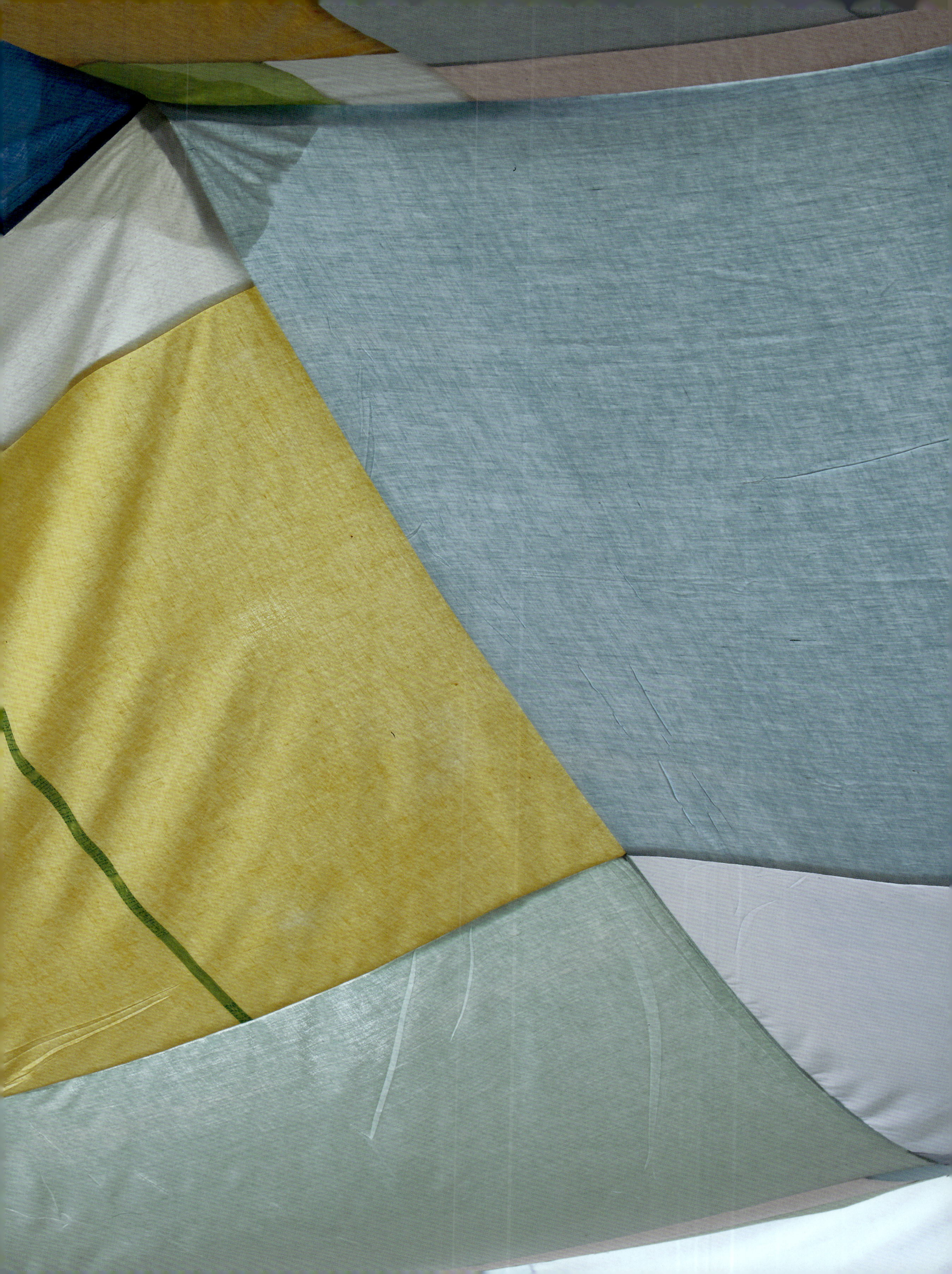

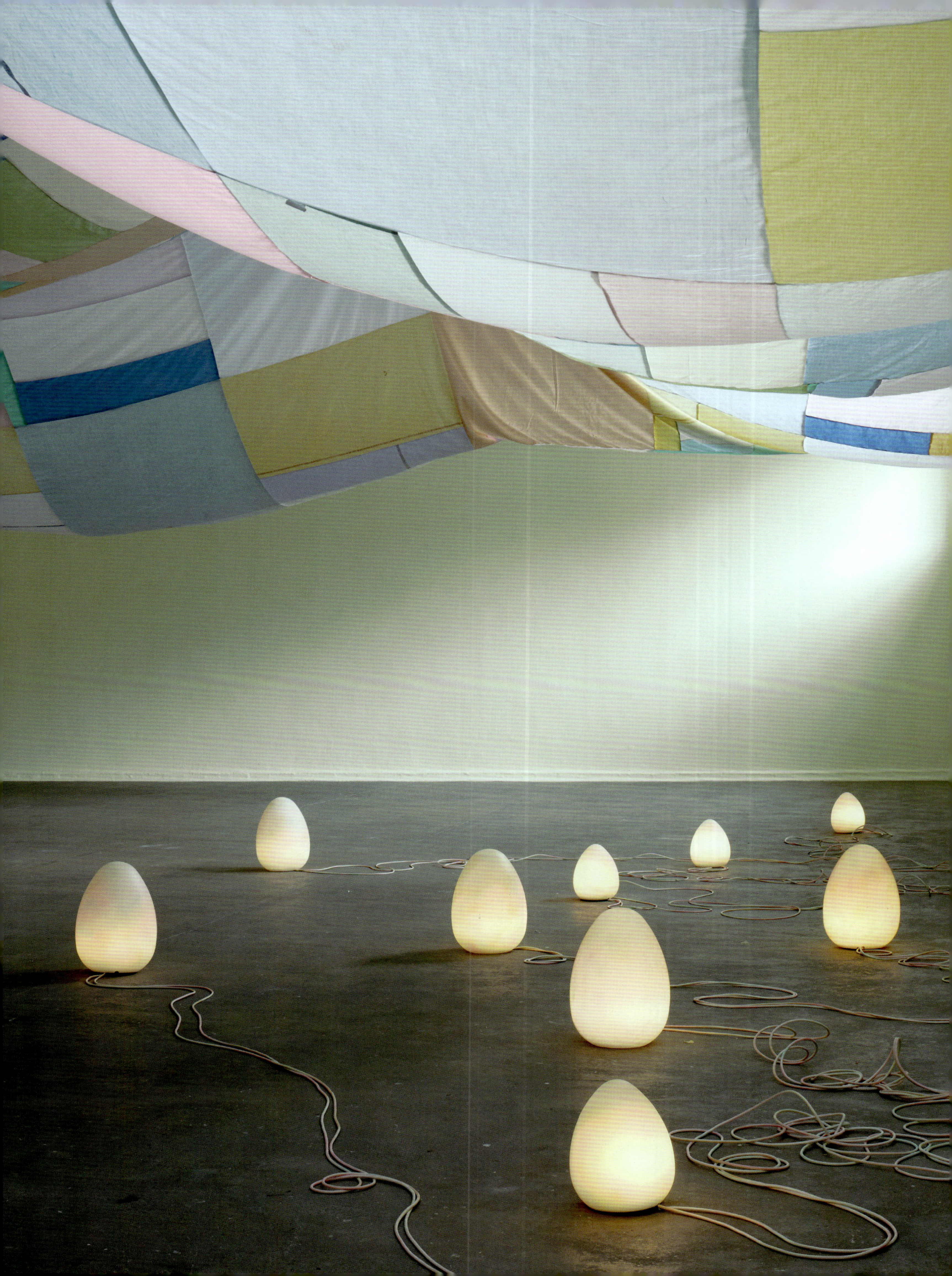

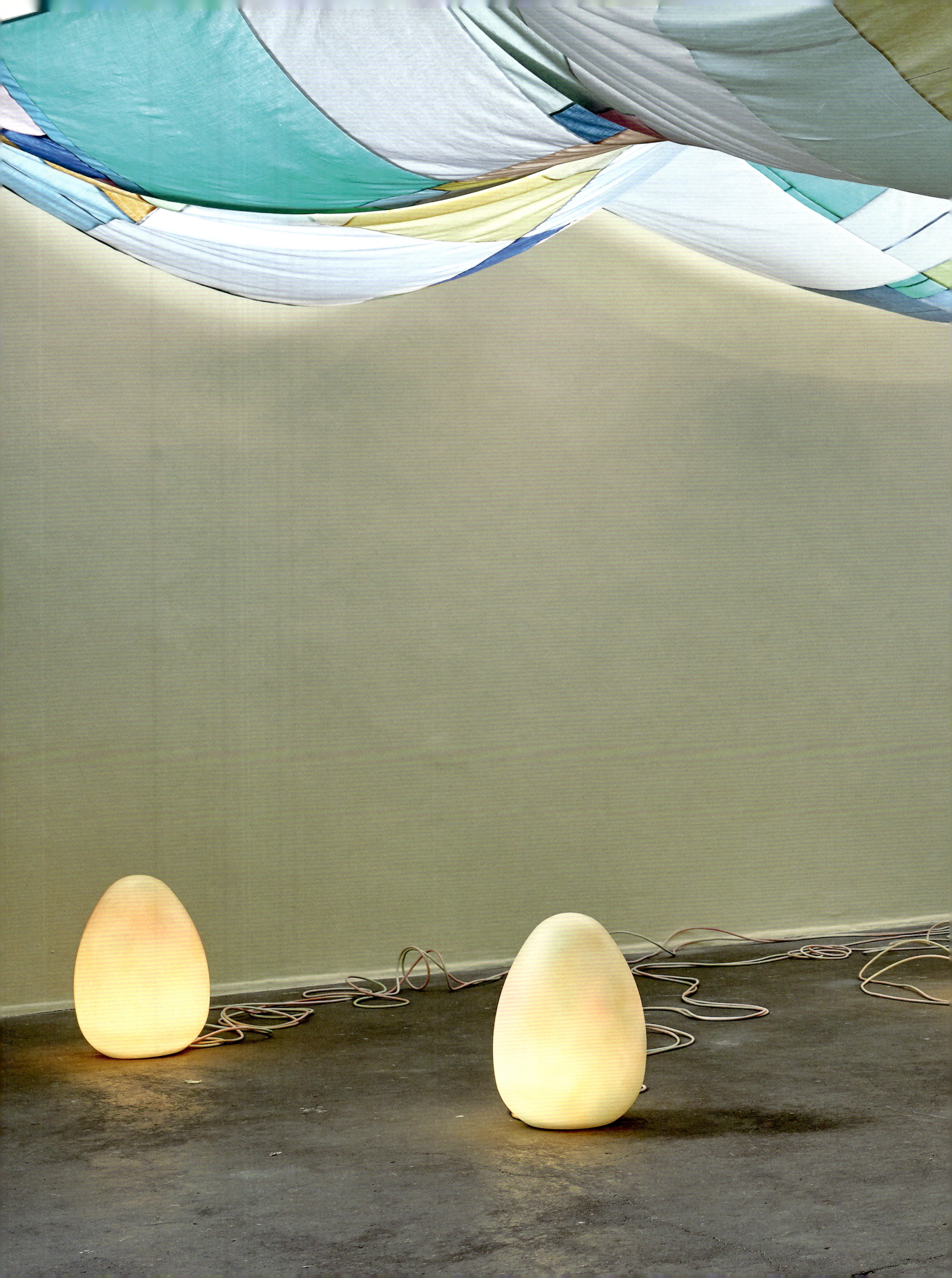

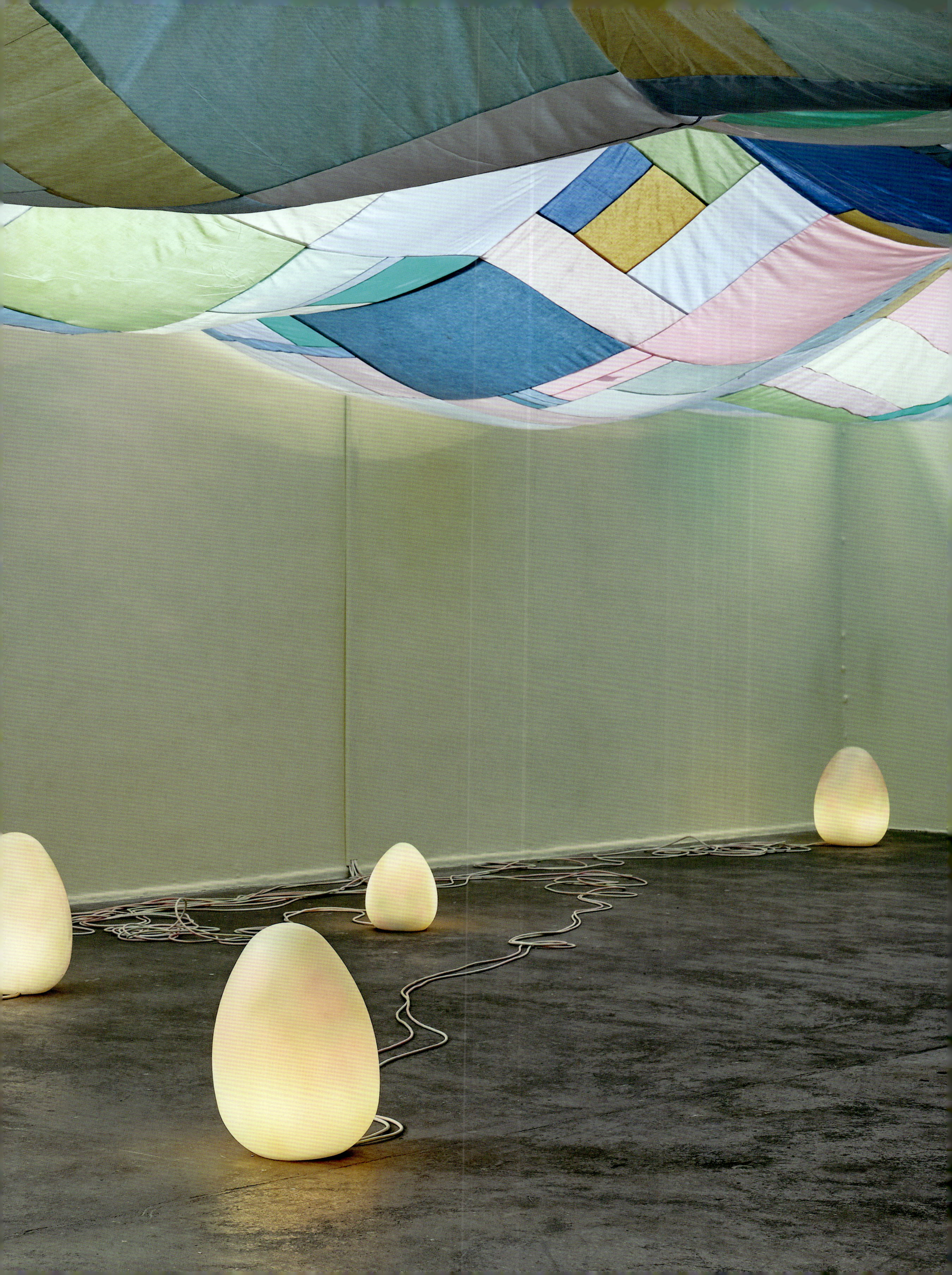

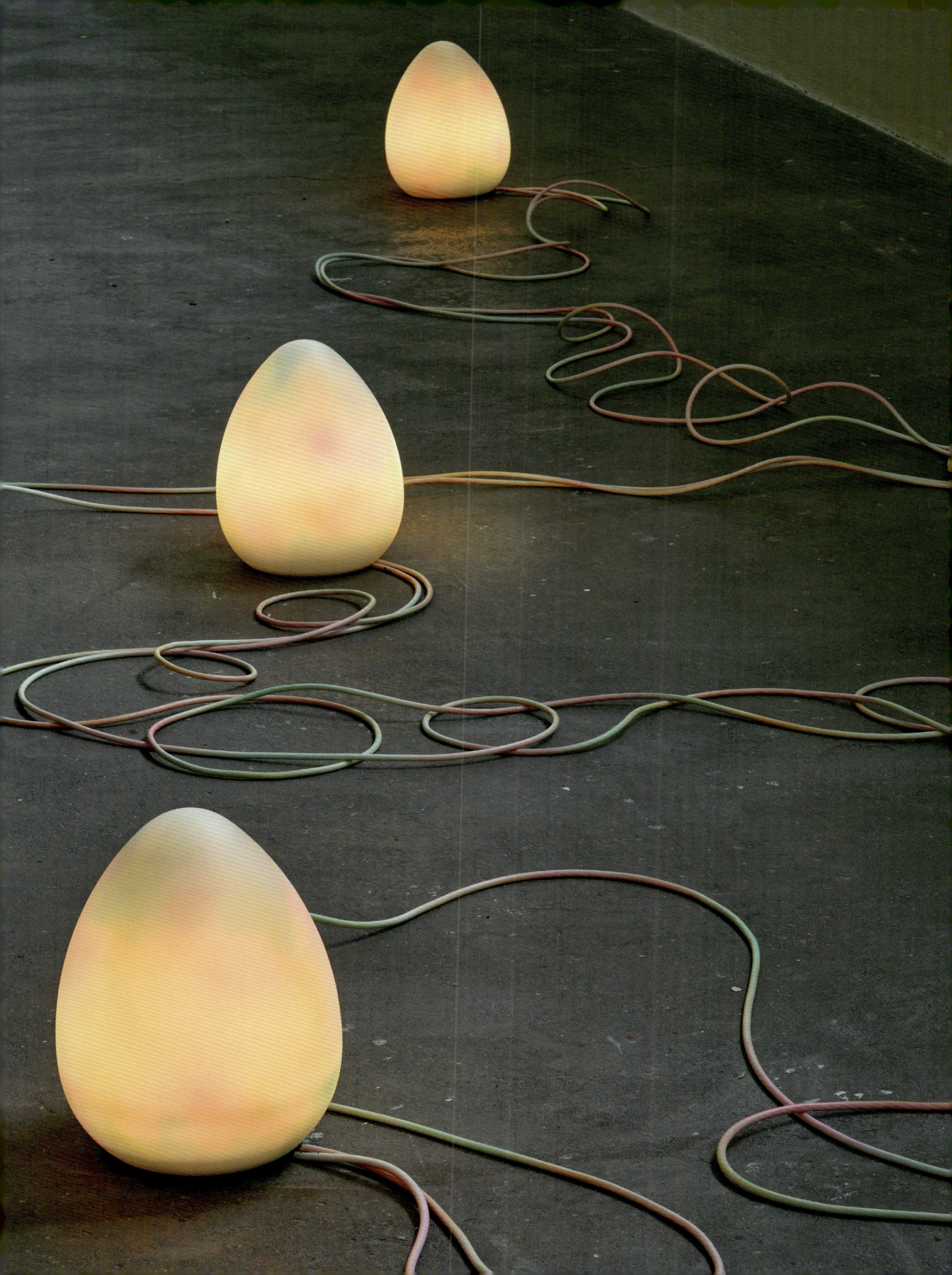

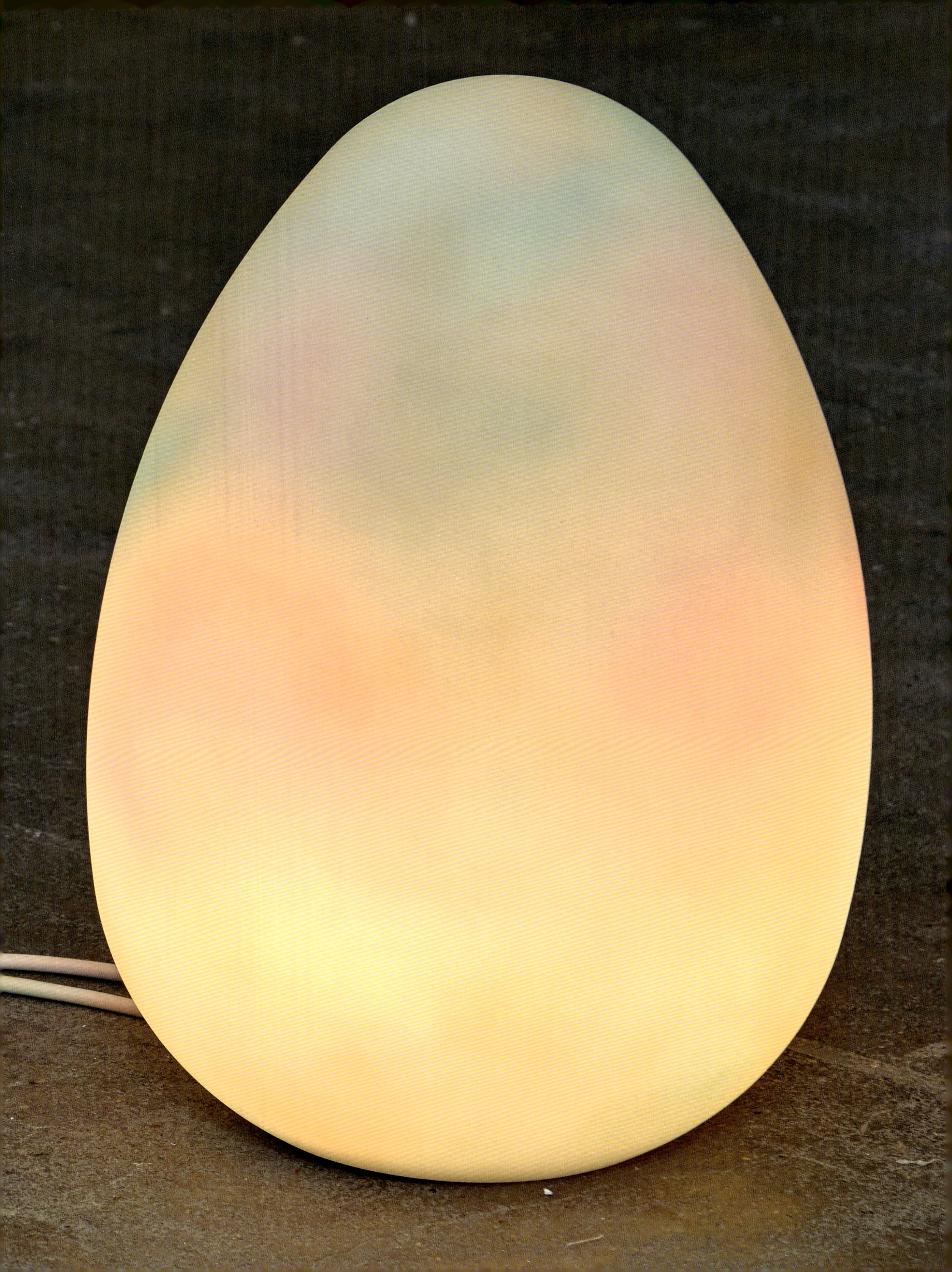

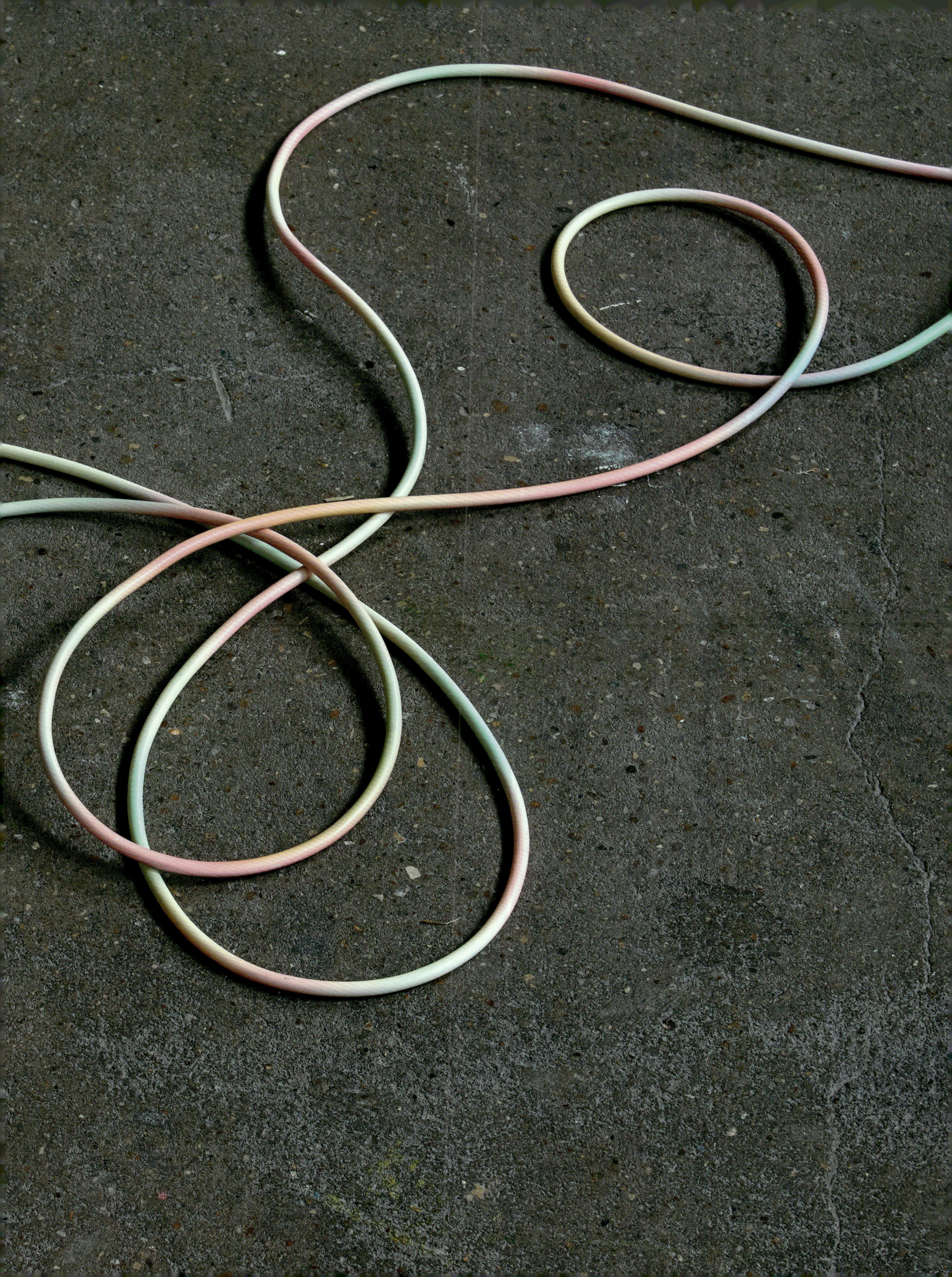

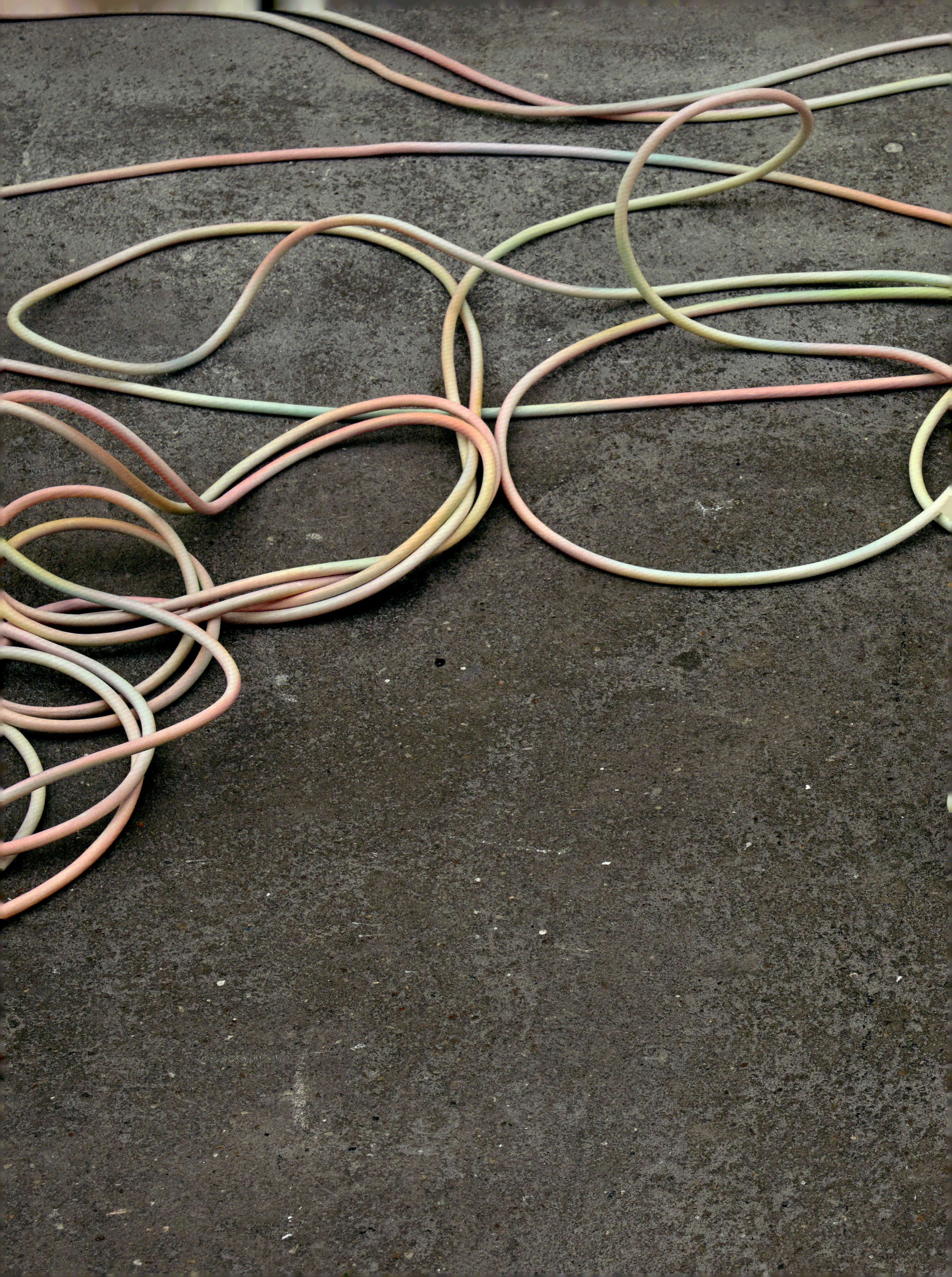

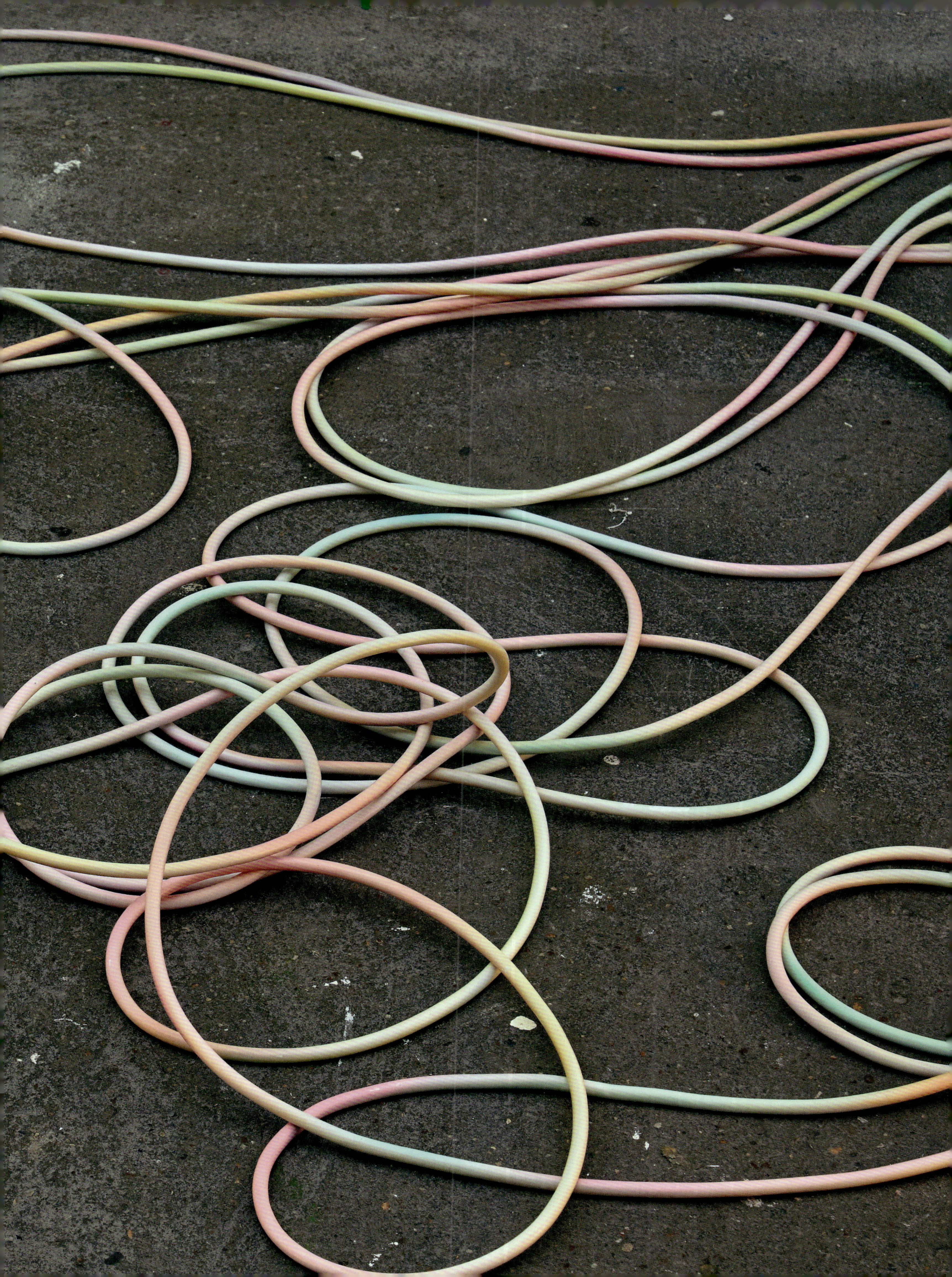

BENOÎT PIÉRON

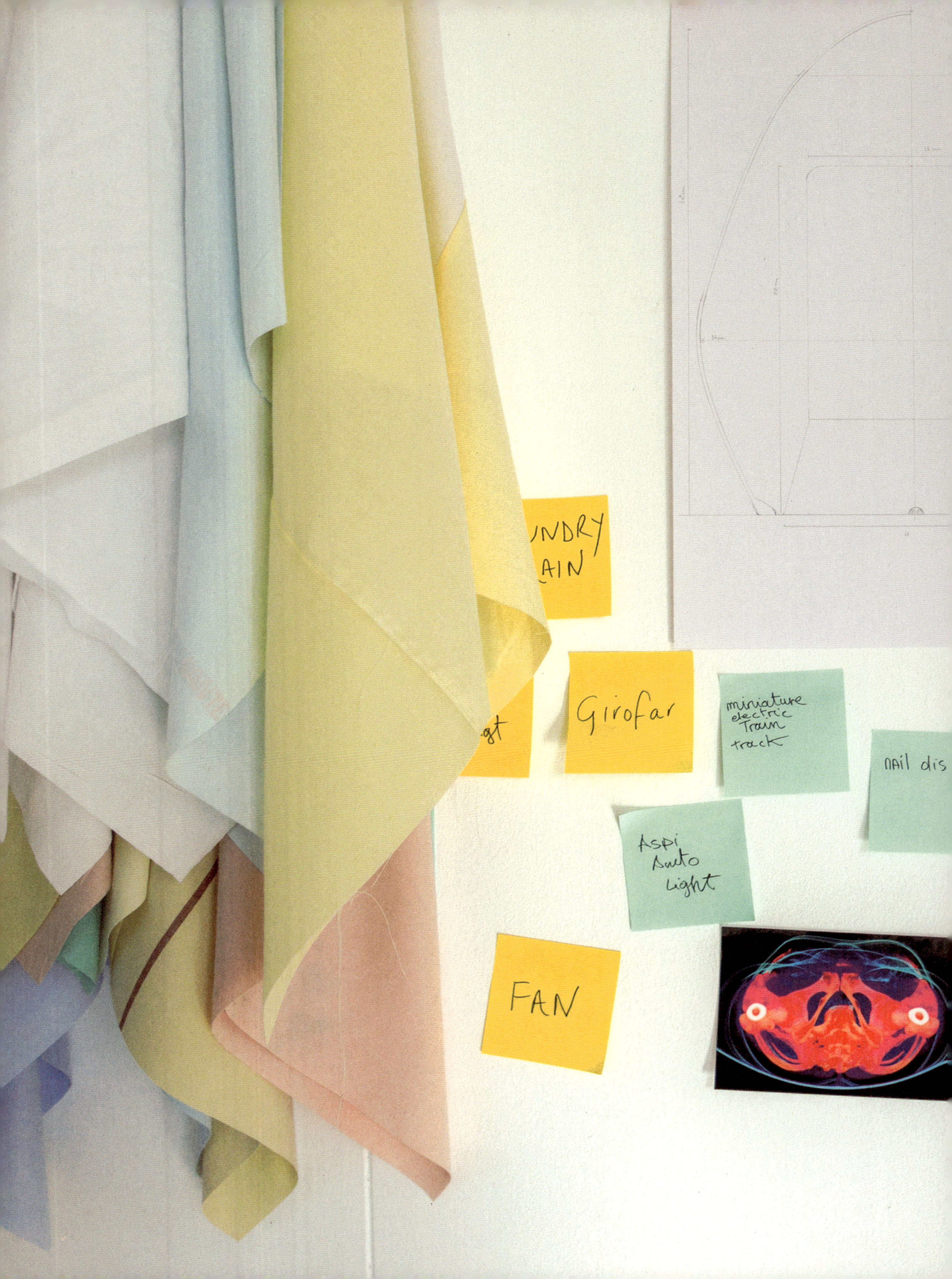

UNDRY
AIN
gt
Girofar
miniature electric Train track
nail dis
Aspi Auto Light
FAN

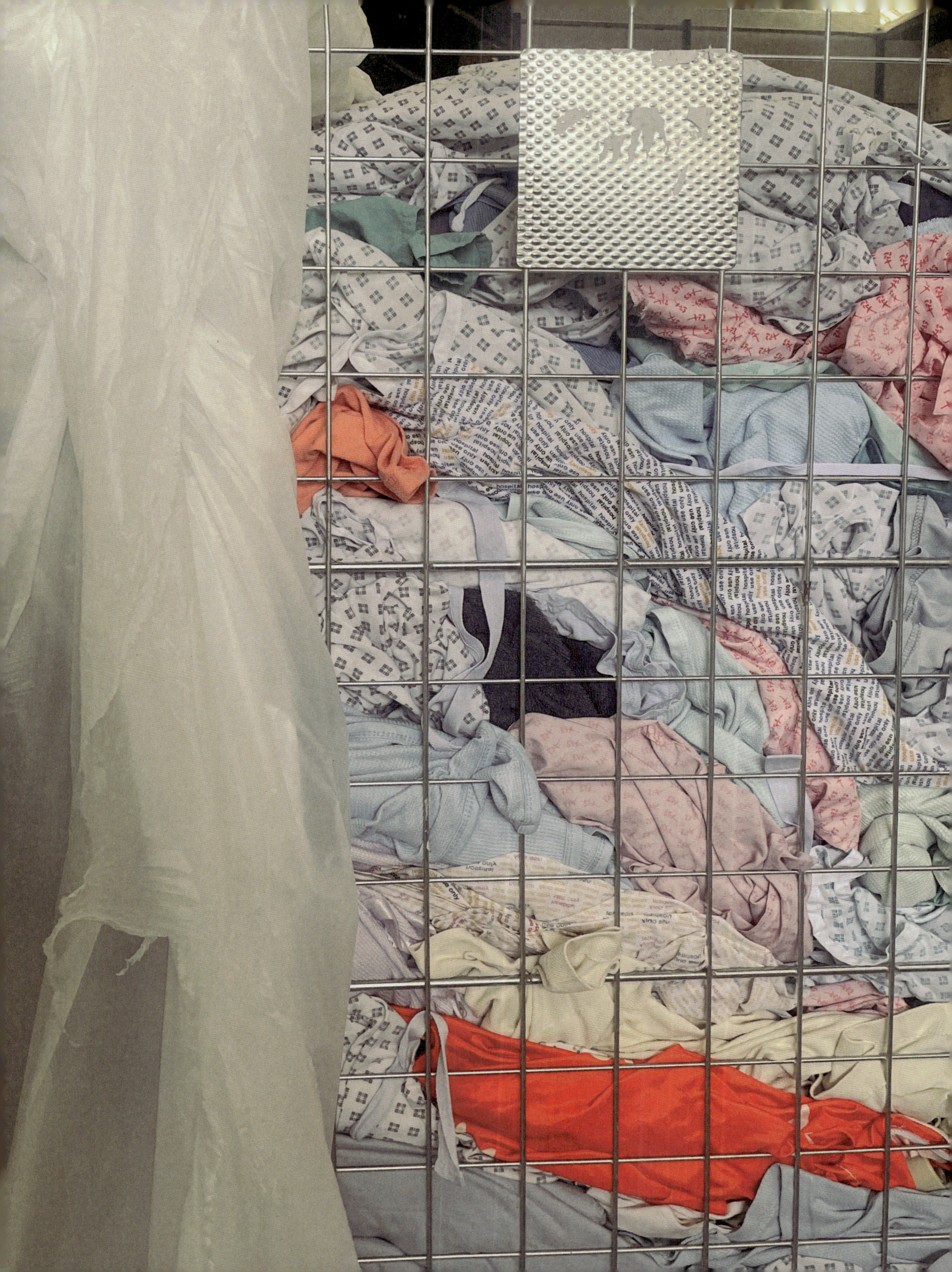
hospital use only

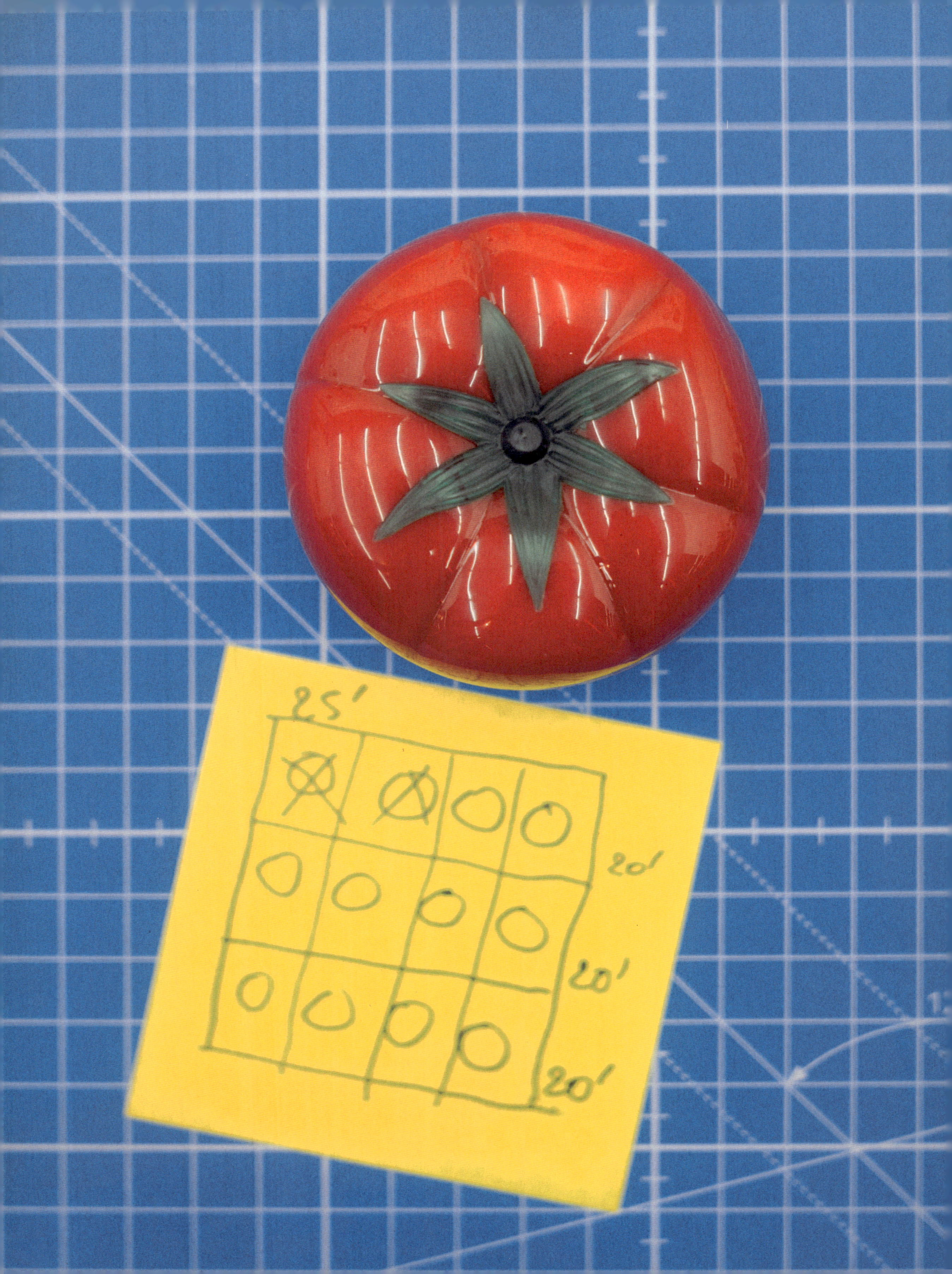
25'
20'
20'
20'

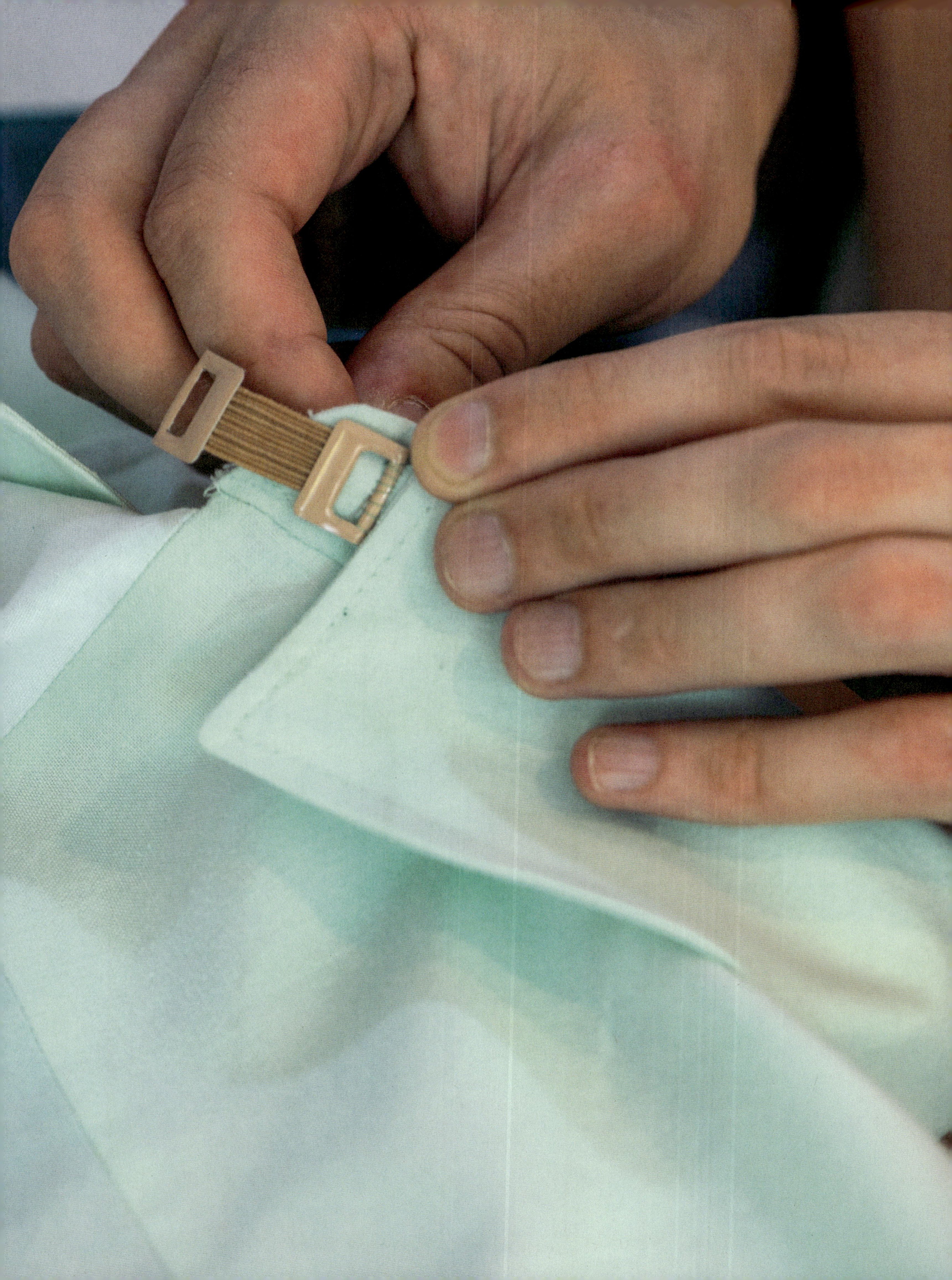

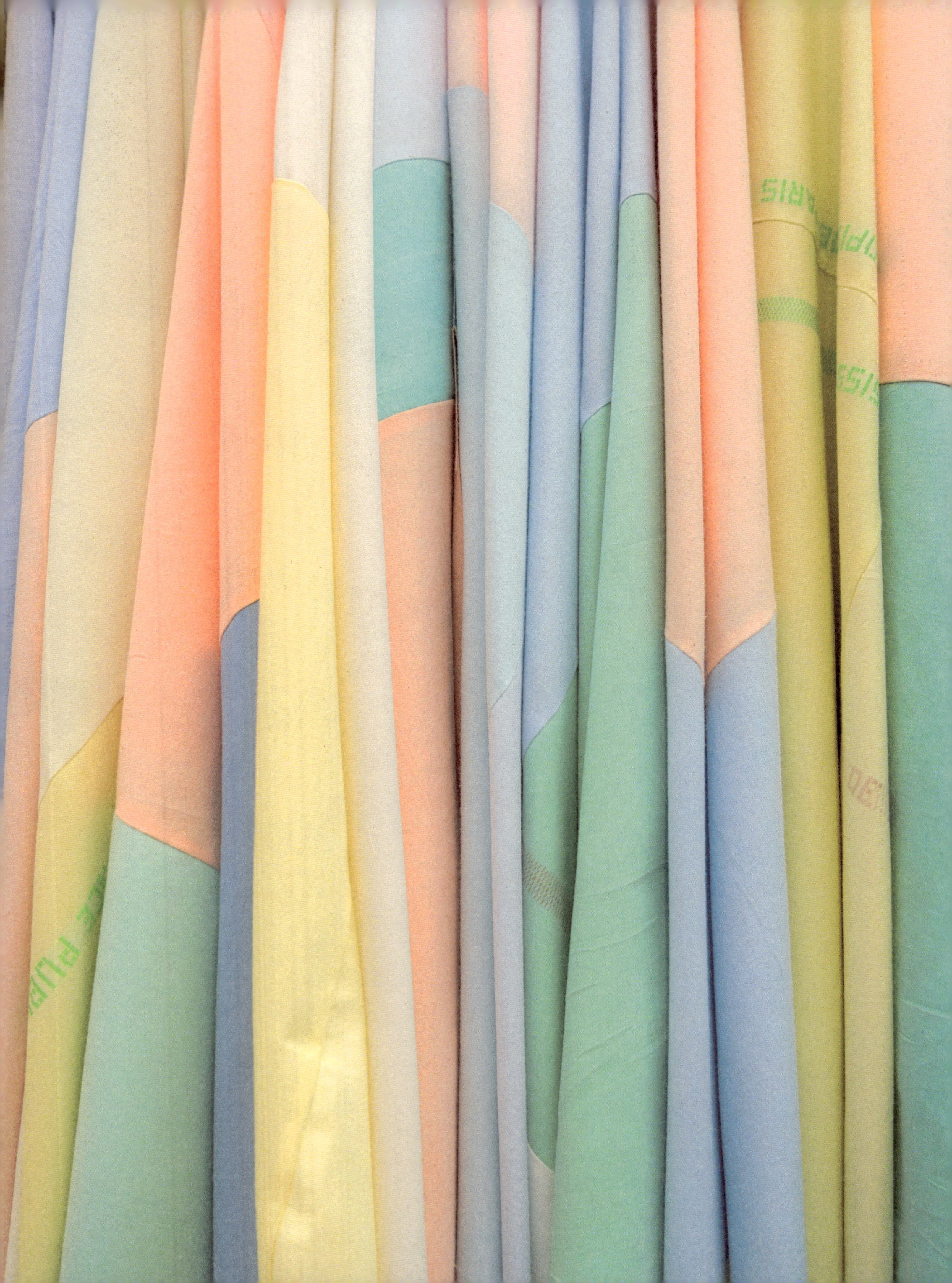

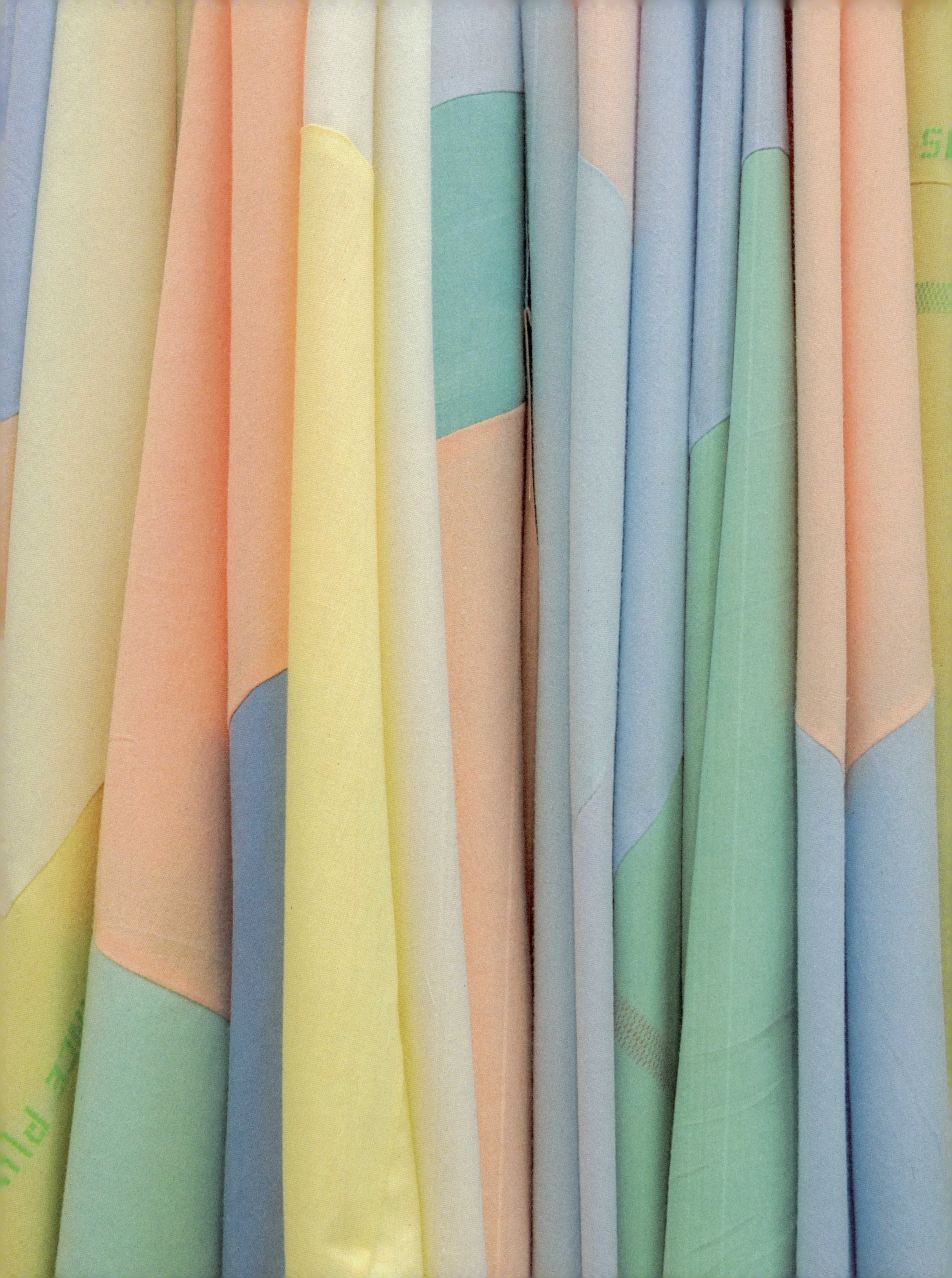

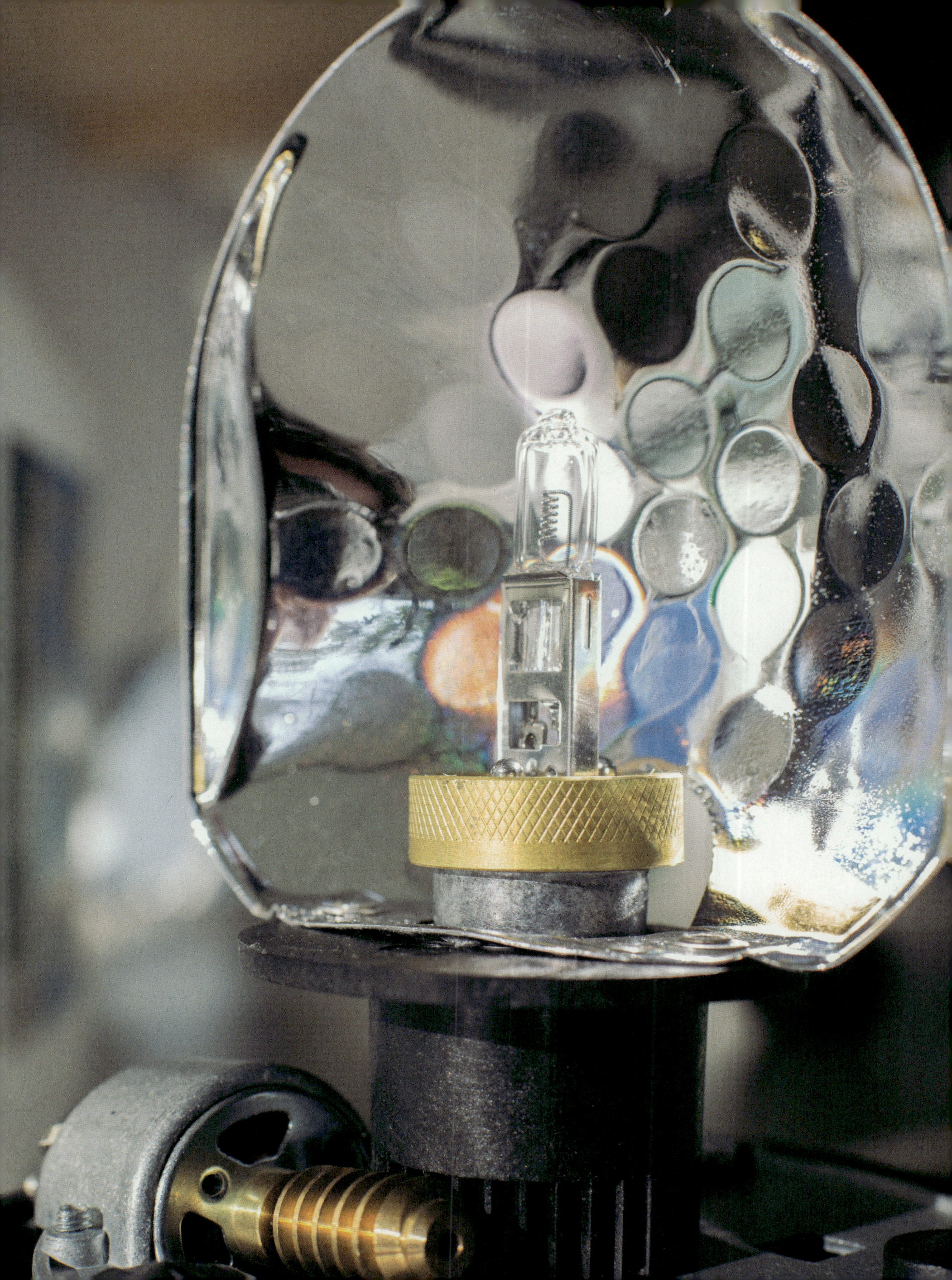

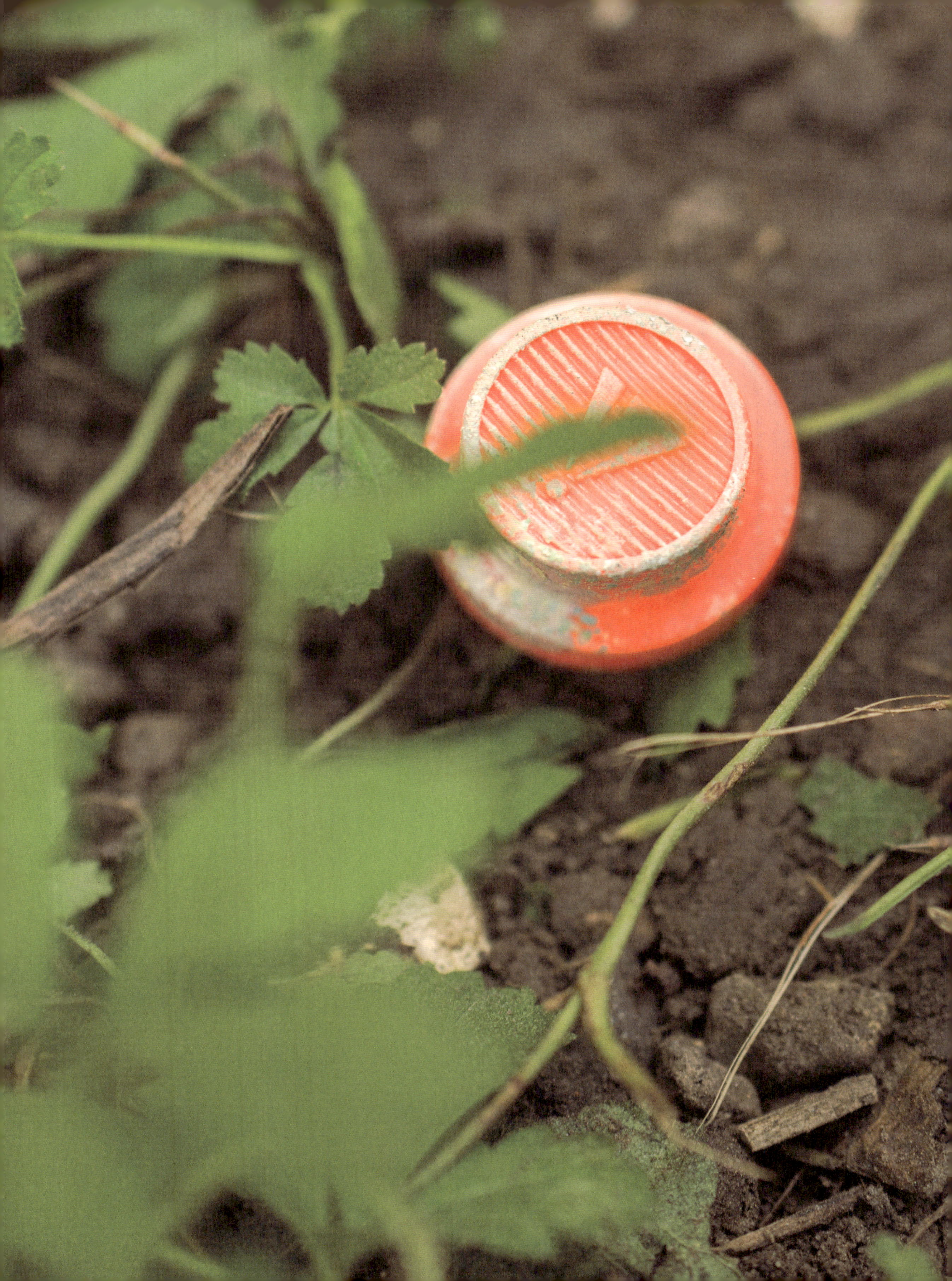

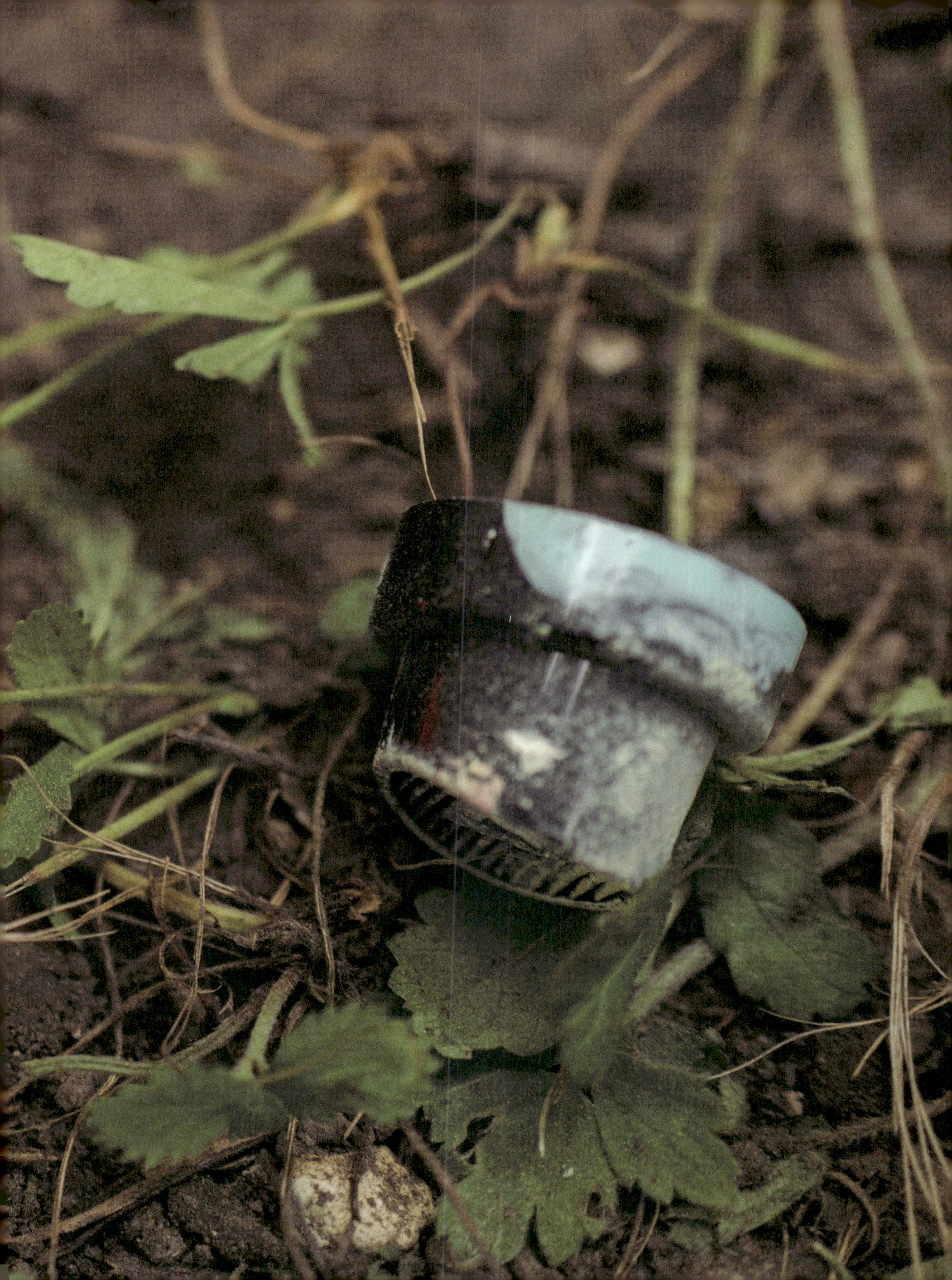

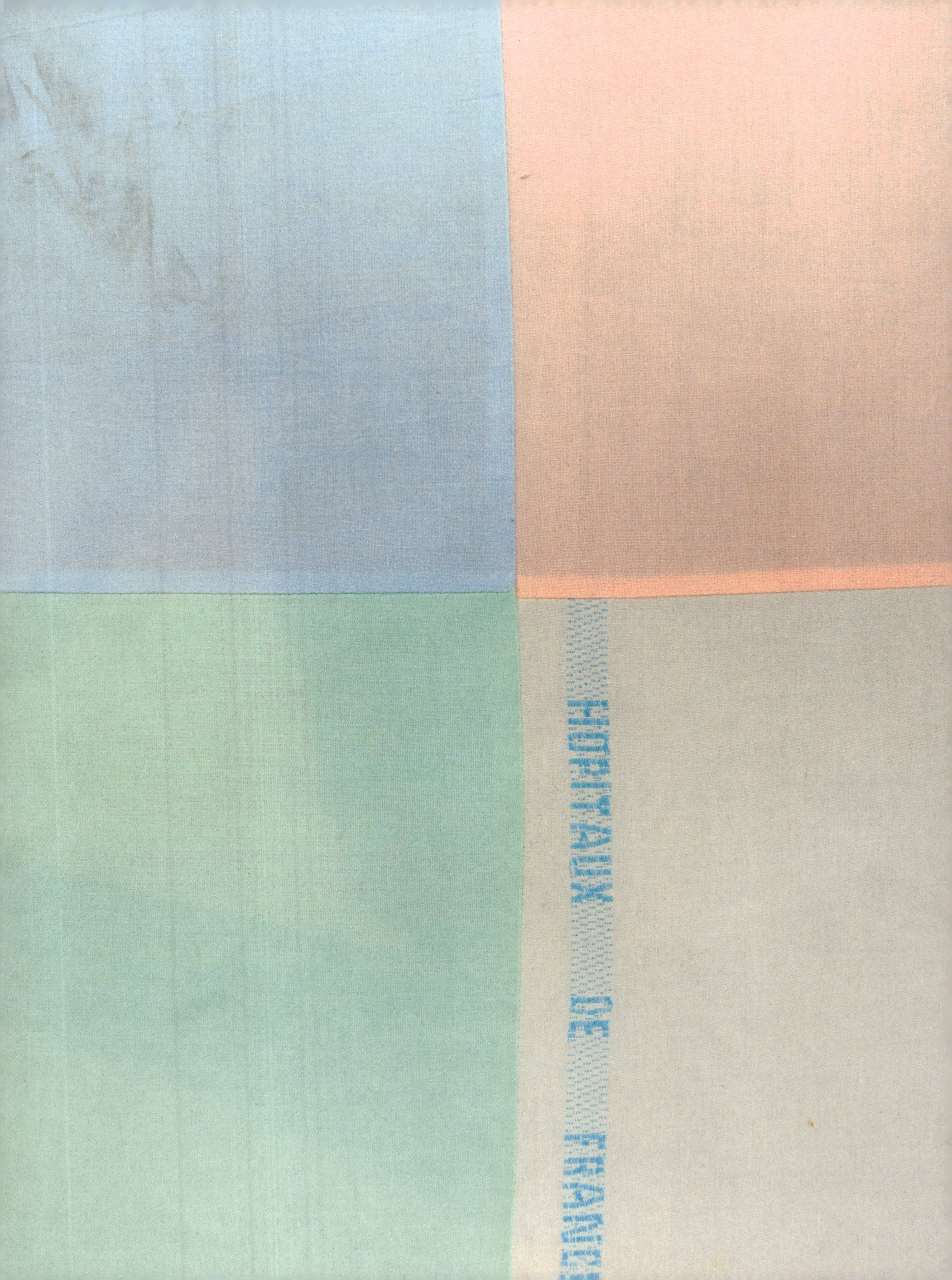
HOPITAUX DE

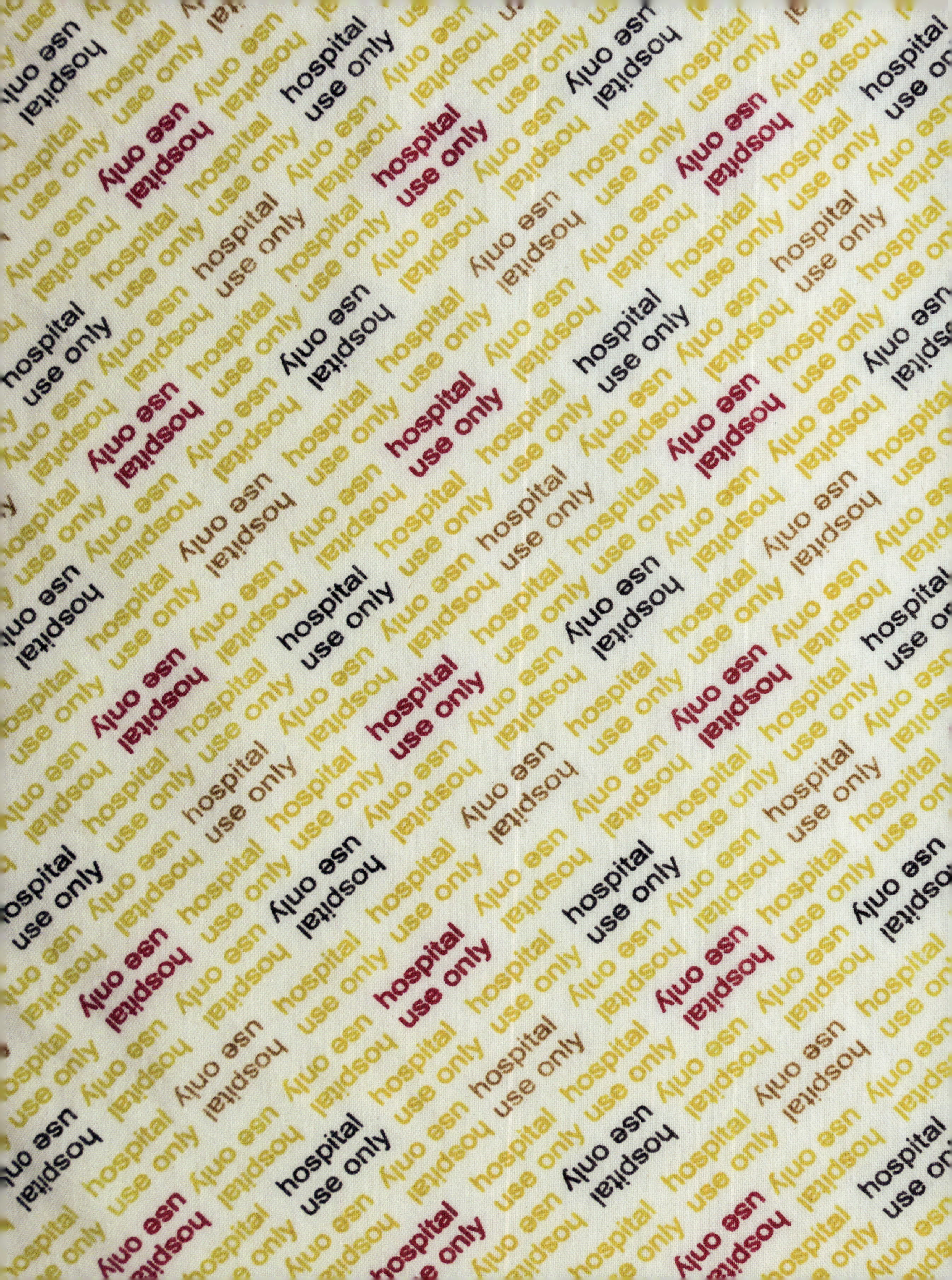
hospital
use only

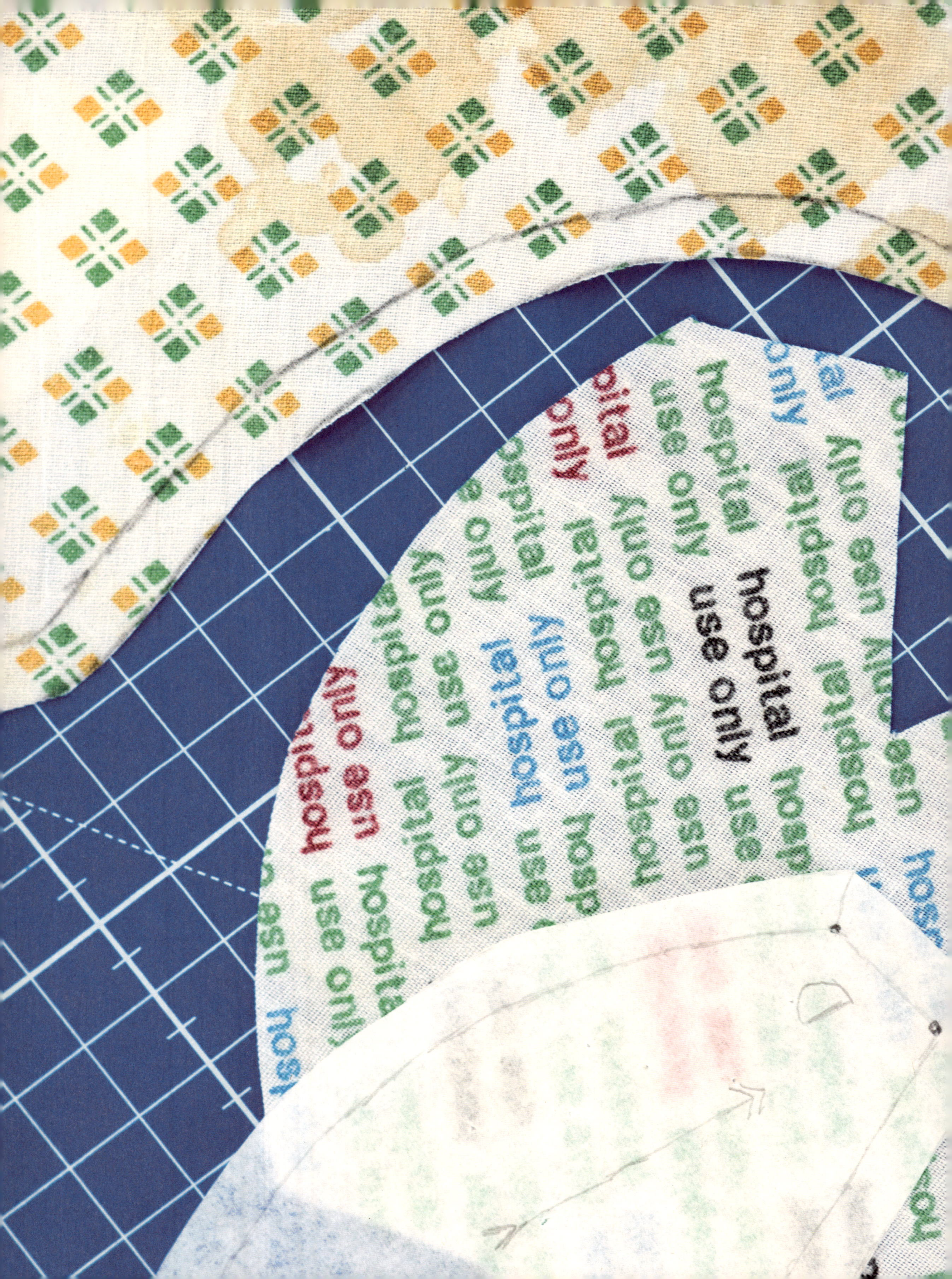
hospital
use only

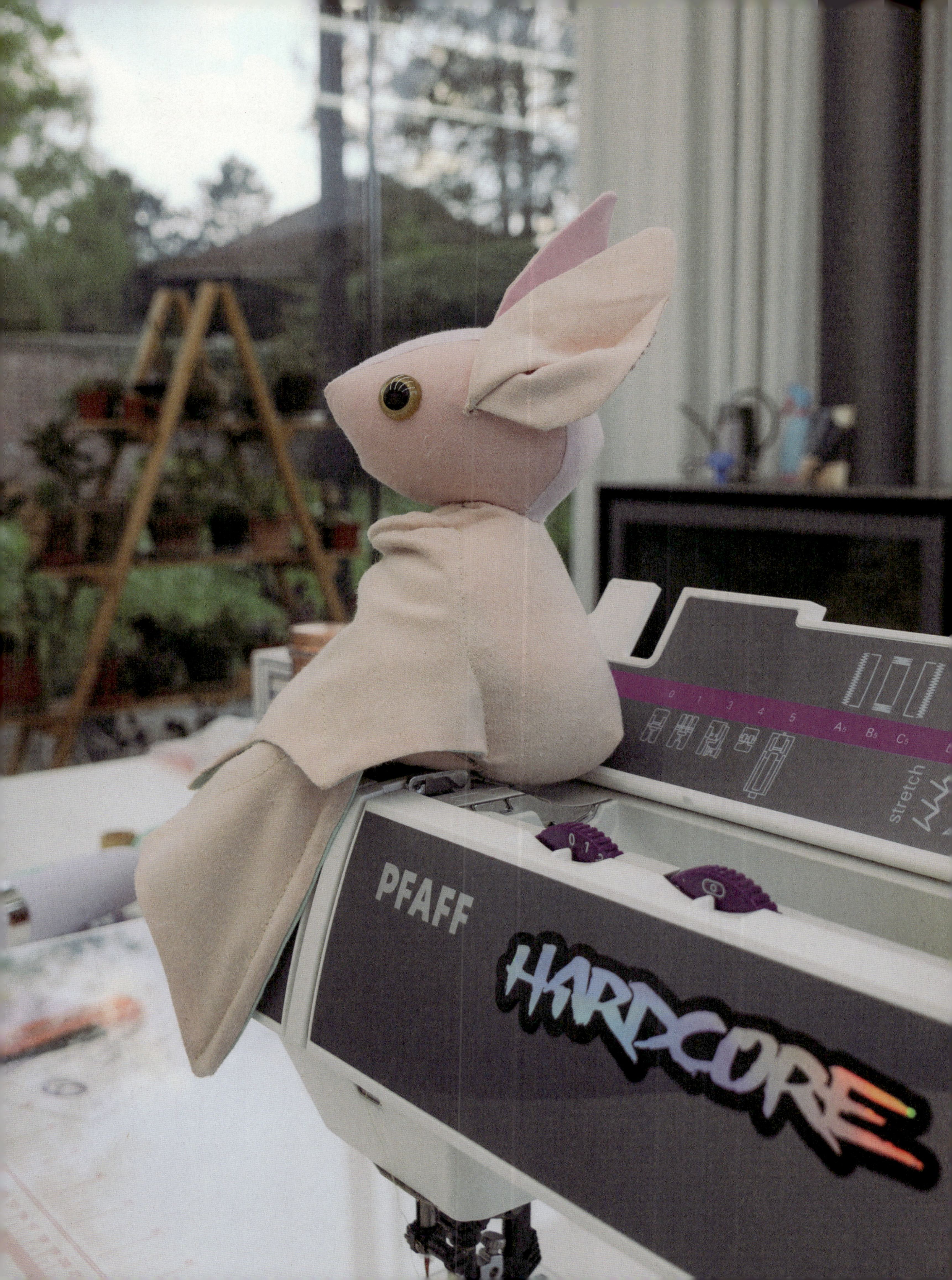
PFAFF
HARDCORE
stretch

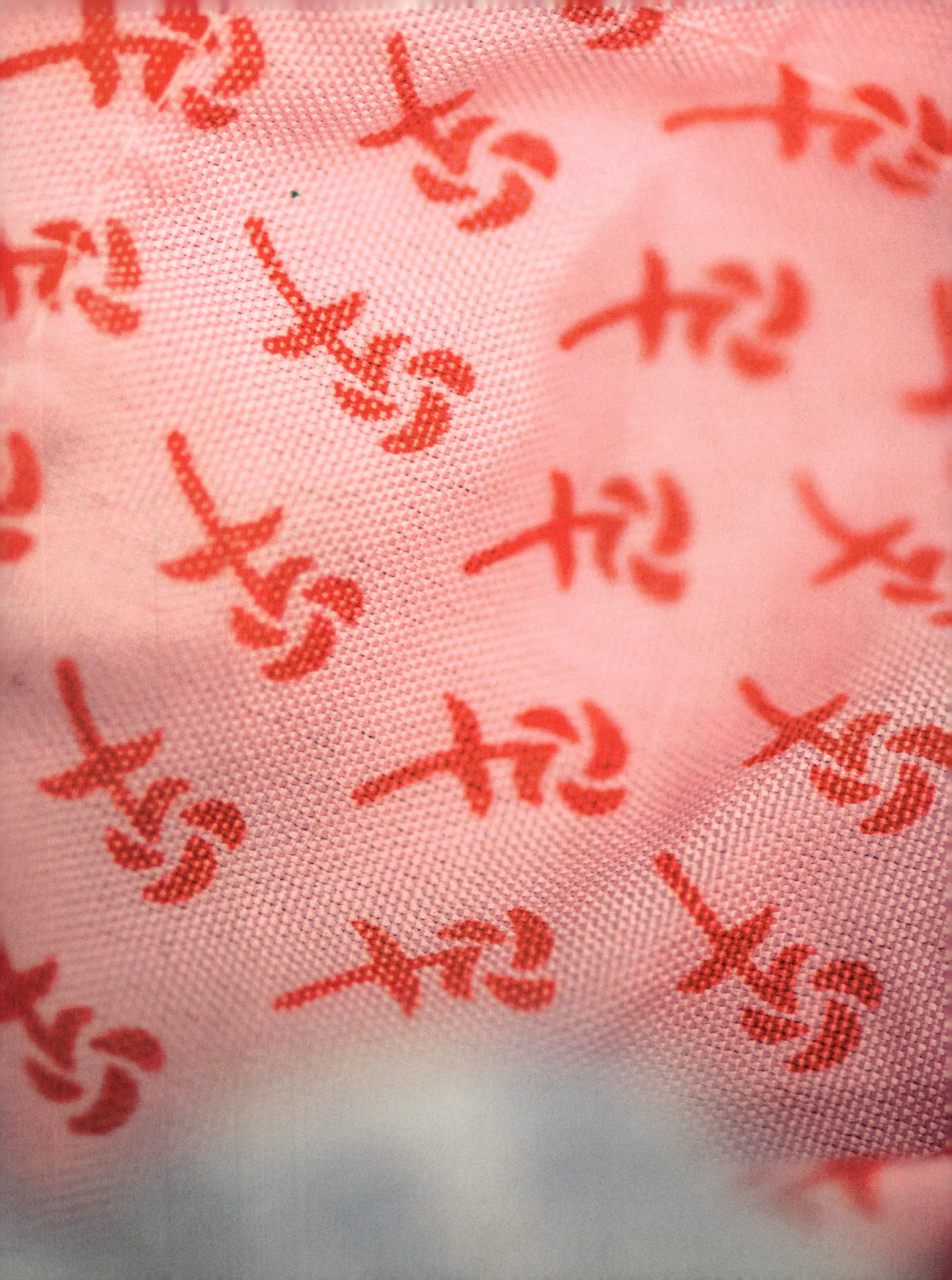

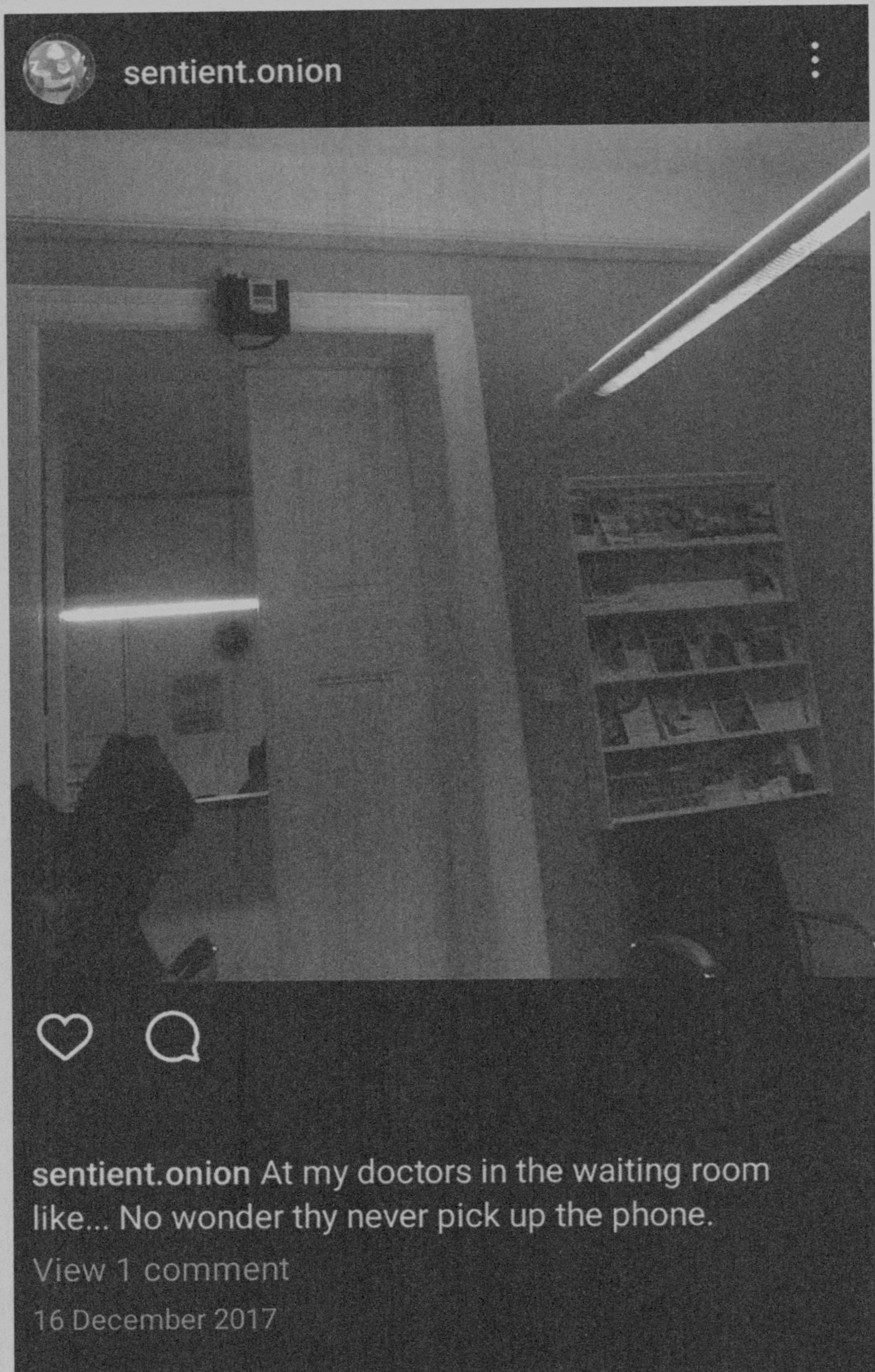

Clay AD (2023). Screenshot. Courtesy of the artist.

NOTES FROM THE OFFICE ACROSS THREE

    P
GLOBAL
    W
    E
    R
    S

CLAY

A
D

GASTROINTESTINAL DOCTOR
BERLIN, 2017

I no longer remember the street the office was on anymore. I think it was Neukölln. Thankfully, I took a photo of the waiting room, where a mysterious telephone hung over the doorway. My German was so basic at that point that I couldn't ask the people at the desk: *Why is that phone there?* I daydreamed about the possible reasons for the phone to distract myself from the dread of seeing this GI doc (I also have zero recollection of his name), who would drop misogynist comments during our appointments for seemingly no reason. However, I had gone through such a process to find someone who would speak English that I couldn't find the energy to switch. No one ever answered the phone, so I usually just tried to come in with a friend to organise my appointments in person. The environment felt pretty unfriendly with one exception. There is a German cultural thing of saying hello when you enter the waiting room. It was curious. In so many spaces in Berlin I found that everyone ignored each other actively and even aggressively, but all waiting together here, for care, we say hello – an acknowledgment of our present shared experience. Unfortunately I always forgot to do it, only remembering once a new person came through the doorway to a chorus of *Hallo*. It felt unnatural, but I liked it. The décor felt like a standard German doctor's office; watercolour paintings of vaguely abstract shapes on the walls, and some plants near the window. The office is in an old apartment, a common setup in Berlin. The rooms echo the floor plan of a domestic environment: the waiting room where the living room used to be, the doctor's office in the bedroom, et cetera. I imagine the ghosts who haunted that building were extremely confused about its present occupiers and energy. That colour orange on the walls though – who had suggested that, and why? It wasn't calming. Maybe they were going for cheerful? It just felt dissonant, like being inside a tangerine while waiting for a colonoscopy.

RILEY CHILDREN'S HOSPITAL
INDIANAPOLIS, 2007

There are paintings of cartoons and landscapes on the walls, like they're trying to cater to an age range of four to eighteen as well as their adult caregivers. It feels un-curated and chaotic. The big waiting room reminds me of a mall. The architecture comprises organic shapes, not geometric ones. The walls are rounded, and the floor plan open except in the corridors that lead to the doctors, who they keep hidden until the last minute. Reflecting on it now, it reminds me of the many buildings in my dreamscape: large, sprawling, holding many rooms and stories, twists and turns. This wing of the children's hospital was relatively new when I was here at fifteen. From a Google search, I see that the outpatient center was rebuilt in 2000. Now, an emergency visit, without insurance, costs $30,000. Sixteen years ago I'm not sure how much it was. Online they say they treat children from families who are unable to pay, but in 2008, when I was kicked off my father's insurance because of preexisting conditions, I can't remember coming back here, so maybe I didn't qualify anymore. Maybe I simply don't remember. All the appointments from that time in my life blend together. I do remember the carpet, with its very swirly pattern of pine green and magenta. I look down at my feet against it, my hightops scribbled on with band lyrics using a ballpoint pen. So many brown couches. This was before smartphones were common, so I'm not sure what my mom was doing with her hands, or what I was doing to pass the time. I imagine I am listening to a CD on my headphones. I can see my teenage face, the boredom masking the anxiety. Mom probably knitting furiously, her hands channeling her anxiety. In my memory, the waiting room is totally empty except for us.

VICTORIA HOSPITAL
PHYSIOTHERAPY DEPARTMENT
GLASGOW, 2023

Posters everywhere. Two cork boards line the walls with posters and information sheets, mostly produced by the NHS. The chairs are really hard, and the environment feels quite sterile, but when I look at the posters, I feel comforted somehow. It reminds me of being at the library: support group meetups, a free citizen's advice hotline for those in debt, interpreter information. I'm certain they have to approve what goes on the cork board. My physio is nice and easygoing. We talk about the *Barbie* movie, which neither of us liked. She sees my chest scars and isn't bothered, just tells me I need to retrain my shoulder from locking up and watches me while I do some exercises. The woman at the desk is sweet, and we make small talk. Austerity is in the air of the hospital, and I know the nurses have recently been on strike; before that it was the ambulance drivers. There is duct tape on the ceiling to cover a hole.

DR. SUSANNE MORATH & DR. HENDRIK SCHÖLL PLASTIC SURGERY
MUNICH, 2020

Expensive. The office smelled, looked, and felt expensive, and my partner, friend, and I got free coffee while we waited. The next day I will get top surgery. This appointment was a short one where the surgeon looked at my chest, drew some lines on my skin, and said, *See you tomorrow*. The office had a few different rooms. All of the walls were made of glass and there were glass sculptures around, as well as oil paintings. Everything was visible at all times except in two of the rooms where there were privacy screens for the patients to get dressed and undressed. This is where the doctor drew on me. The others in the waiting room were a mix of trans people and cis people. I kind of loved the extreme weirdness of the situation, even though I felt pretty anxious. Everyone in the office was super friendly. I got the surgery paid for by insurance, but because plastic surgery is the big money of health care, you get treated like a customer rather than a patient. Nine days later, the day after I arrived back in Berlin, the German government would declare a lockdown for COVID-19, but I didn't know that yet. That day I was simply sitting, holding my partner's hand, wondering how many procedures translated to the worth of the giant, fucking ugly painting in the waiting room, and trying not to think about how the next day, I'd wake up with a completely new chest.

MY HOUSE
GLASGOW, 2021

I am waiting to speak to my new gastrointestinal doctor in Glasgow. Two years on, I still have not met him, but I've become familiar with his soft Irish accent over the phone. I waited for the unlisted call, which is the appointment. If I miss it, I wait for him to call back. If I miss it a few times, he'll give up and then I have to wait for a letter to get another appointment a few months later. Like many things in the NHS, the process is not personal. My phone is temperamental, so I often miss the first call, sometimes all of them. Today I answer the second attempt. He asks where in America I'm from, and we speak about the Midwest. I ask where he's from in Ireland, and we speak about Cork. He doesn't judge me for taking myself off my immune-suppressing drugs during COVID. The waiting room is my living room and the doctor's office. I sit between the intimacy of his voice in my ear and the realisation that we will probably never meet.

WAITING ROOM ACTIVITIES

P
MAHEKE
U
L

M
ROXANNE
I
L
L
E
T

CLAY

A
D

B
E
N
PIÉRON
Î
T

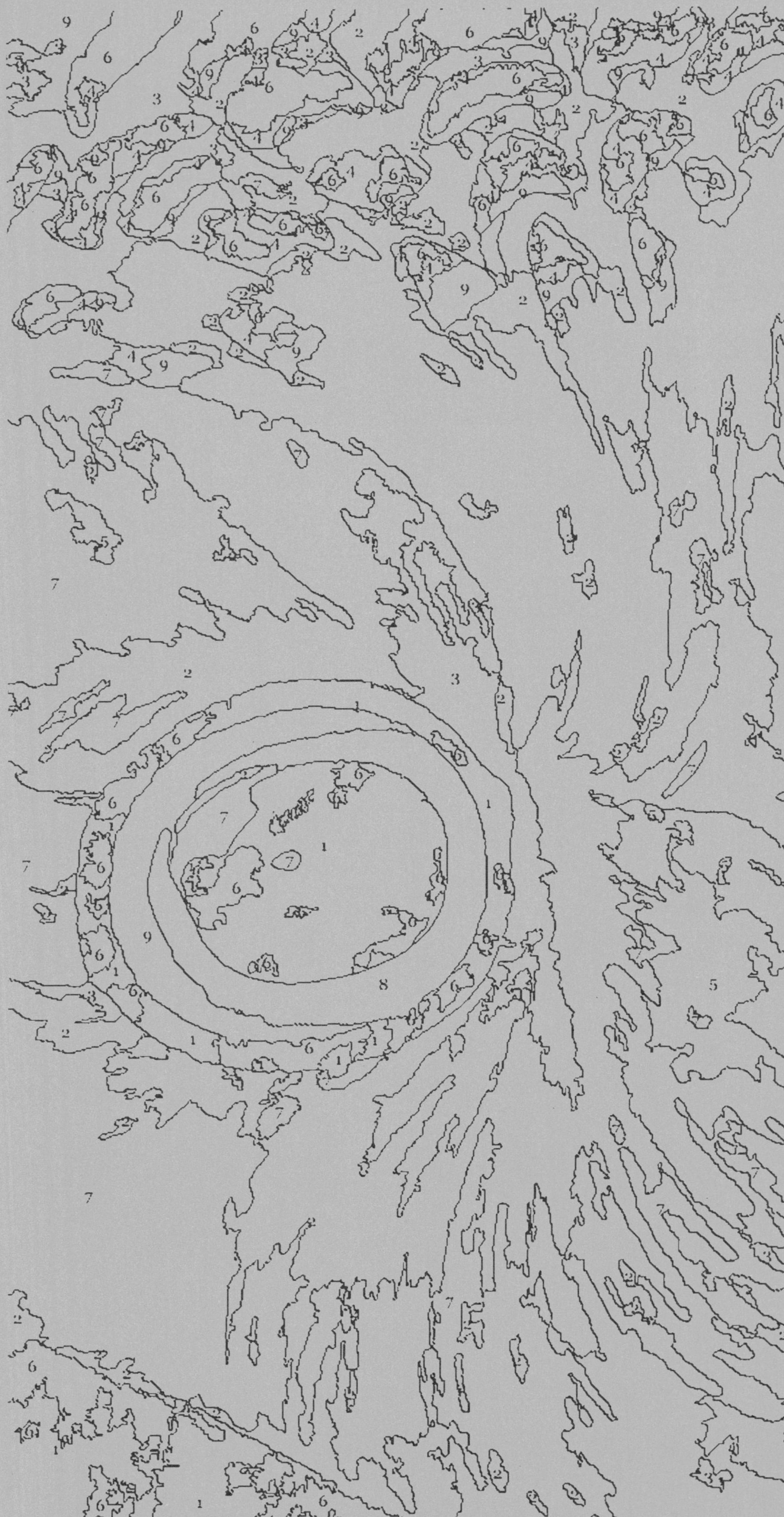

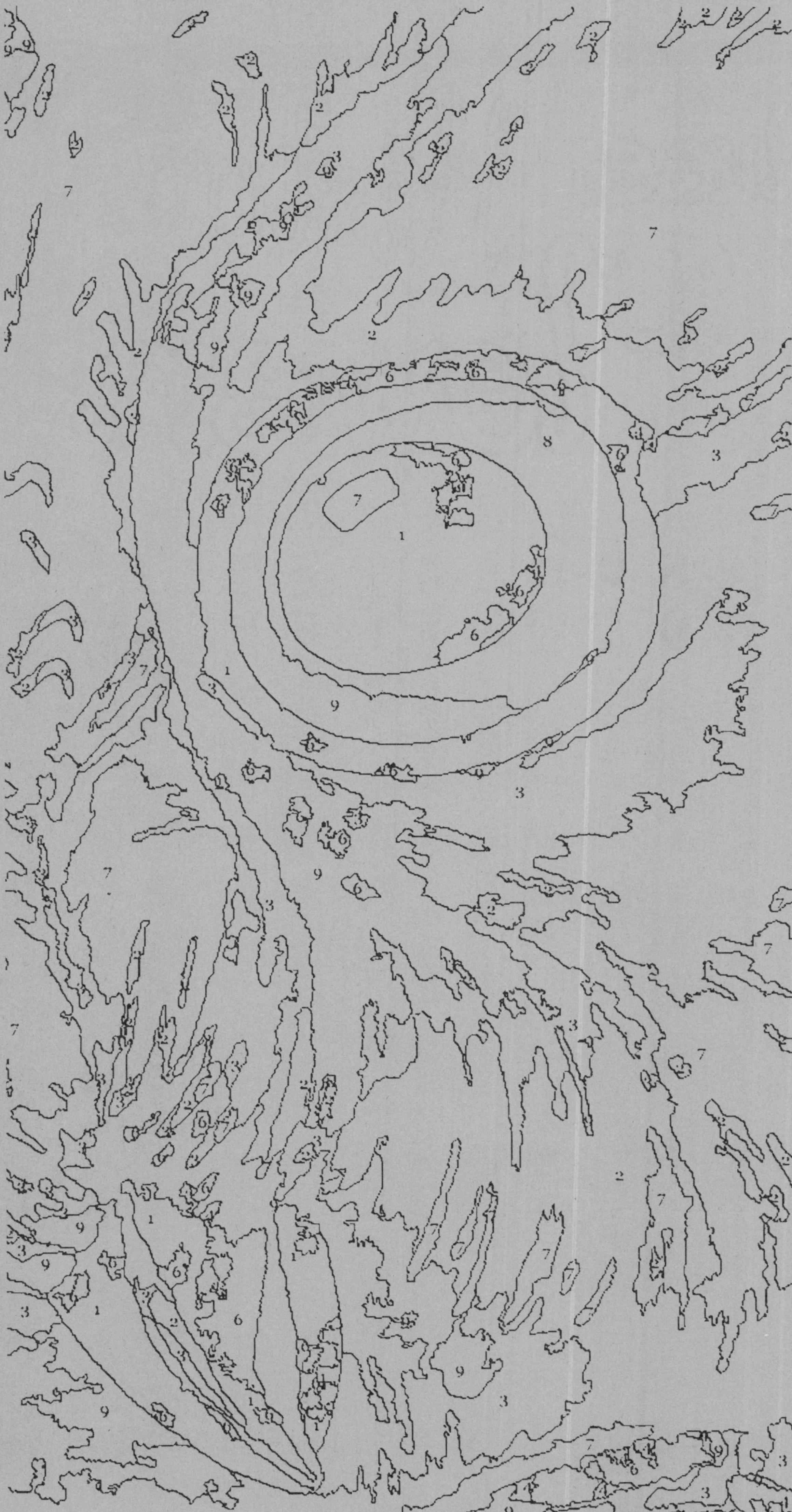

A Queer History Of Flowers

V	I	O	L	A	A	S	U	R	A	S	R	S	H
A	M	P	R	S	N	U	E	S	E	T	U	B	U
M	D	U	O	I	A	H	S	A	N	L	I	T	S
A	U	R	T	A	Y	T	C	M	L	A	A	H	U
R	S	U	L	G	O	N	M	B	S	V	G	I	H
A	H	Y	P	E	R	I	C	U	M	A	R	B	T
N	E	B	U	S	E	C	N	C	V	N	A	I	N
T	C	T	E	G	B	A	E	U	L	D	V	S	A
H	A	U	S	L	A	Y	O	S	R	U	E	C	I
U	U	T	A	L	L	H	M	N	L	L	O	U	D
S	I	A	M	L	A	U	A	U	V	A	&	M	Y
U	M	N	A	I	H	A	S	N	E	R	E	E	A
N	L	K	U	A	R	O	G	A	R	D	N	A	M
S	N	A	R	C	I	S	S	U	S	A	S	A	A

sambucus
hypericum
amaranthus
narcissus
mandragora
ruta graveolens
bellus
lavandula
viola
dianthus
hyacinthus
hibiscum
rosa

LAVENDER

Shades of purple have been used by LGBTQ communities since the days of Sappho. However, lavender truly became an integral part of the gay vocabulary toward the late 19th century. Why this specific shade? Some speculate it's due to its mixing up of pink and blue. Others trace its connection to notions of effeminacy in history. The visibility of the color lavender among the queer community received another surge when individuals participating in a "gay power" march in New York City in 1969. This occurred a month after the significant Stonewall Riots. In that year, Betty Friedan, who led the National Organization for Women, expressed concern about lesbian members, perceiving them as a potential threat to feminism. She labeled this perceived threat the "lavender menace" – a vivid and multi-faceted term that lesbian activists promptly embraced as part of their own identity.

ROSES

In Japanese history, the rose has held a connection with gay men. The term for rose in Japanese, pronounced as "bara," underwent a renewed presence in queer media during the 1960s and 1970s. The inaugural commercially published gay magazine in Japan, originating in 1971, bore the title "Barazoku," which translates to "rose tribe." Roses, particularly when displayed in various colors or embellished with a spectrum of rainbow hues, stand as a favored flower choice for Pride events.

PANSIES

The term "pansy" is commonly recognized as a derogatory label for a gay man, carrying connotations of fragility and effeminacy. (Interestingly, actual pansy flowers are quite resilient.) In Marcel Proust's "Sodome et Gomorrhe," the concept of male-male courtship was likened to the process of flower fertilization. In this context, men were playfully referred to as "evening botanists," "buttercups," or "horticultural lads." While the late 19th century confined gay male interactions to the shady red-light district beneath the elevated train tracks of the Bowery, and kept lesbian existence predominantly hidden within private salons for privileged women, the era of prohibition marked the initial emergence of a noticeable gay and lesbian community. Prohibition necessitated a mingling of diverse individuals, all seeking the same prohibited beverage, which in turn fostered a culture of moderate acceptance, if not complete permissiveness. This transformation brought attention to the outdated moral stance of the Temperance movement. Consequently, numerous historical gay bars adopted names like "The Pansy Club."

VIOLETS

Sappho who resided on the island of Lesbos around 630-570 BC, frequently alluded to violets in her ancient verses, establishing a connection with love between women. Young girls would playfully decorate themselves with garlands, wearing numerous "crowns of violets." "**You put on many wreaths of violets and roses ... together by my side, and round your tender neck you put many woven garlands made from flowers.**" Similar to lavender, violets experienced a resurgence as a representation of queerness during the early 20th century. This resurgence was attributed to gatherings of women in Paris who revitalized interest in the writings of Sappho. Within this group, known as the "Paris Lesbos," was Renee Vivien, a British poet, who extensively employed the symbolism of violets in her creative output and her individual style. She used violets as a dual homage to Sappho and one of her own romantic partners Natalie Clifford Barney.

grEEn Carnation

Selecting a green carnation as a symbol might appear unusual, yet the individual who brought it into prominence was regarded as peculiar as well. Oscar Wilde, an Irish writer renowned for his romantic involvements with men, employed green carnations to generate excitement during the debut of his play "Lady Windermere's Fan" in 1892. Wilde requested both actors and admirers to give these flowers, without providing an explanation. Historical accounts propose that he might have adopted this trend from Paris, where green carnations were rumored to signify association within the gay male community.

Inner Child/ren:

in the waiting room our inner child/ren can easily get activated. Some preventative tools to nurture these parts of ourselves are:

- ★ bringing a friend/support to your appointment or planning to check in with them after the appointment or by text while waiting so you do not feel alone
- ★ a stuffed animal, small rock, special object or wearing comforting piece of clothing
- ★ snacks and water
- ★ something destracting to read/watch/listen to

RAGE &

LISTENING TO THE ACTIVATED INNER CHILD:

put hand to chest, stomach or whereever feels comforting to notice your own touch. Feel the warmth of your hand Notice if the touch feels soothing, if it does continue - if not push into floor & try one of the suggestions for stress.

MEDITA STRATEGI THE WA

dissociation:

dissociation is a superpower many of us are intimately familiar with. It allows us to check out of overwhelming situations; the doctors office is a place where it is often times safer for those of us with medical trauma to dissociate than be present. light forms of dissociation include scrolling on the phone, heavier forms can feel like leaving your body &/or difficulty being verbal - but dissociation also looks different for everyone.

if you notice yourself dissociating in the waiting room & you'd like to gently come back you can try gently pressing your feet into the floor & looking around the room & noticing what you see and describing it in your head ex: the red chair, a potted plant, a magizine stand etc...

STRESS + ANXIETY:

TRY MOVINC

FINDING A FOCUS F

SOME MIGHT WORK BETT THAN OTHERS; EXAMPL

- ★ THE SEAT U
- ★ YOUR FEET ON
- ★ A SOUND/S IN OR OUTSIDE
- ★ PERSON, PLACE NONHUMAN T
- ★ NOTICING THE OF SOMETHING

ANGER:

RAGE + ANGER IS A VERY NORMAL FEELING AS A PATIENT. SOME STRATEGIES TO MOVE THIS ENERGY ARE:

- ★ go to bathroom + scream silently
- ★ push on a wall, in the bathroom or hallway
- ★ tell yourself you aknowledge and honor this rage and need to bookmark it until it can safely be expressed

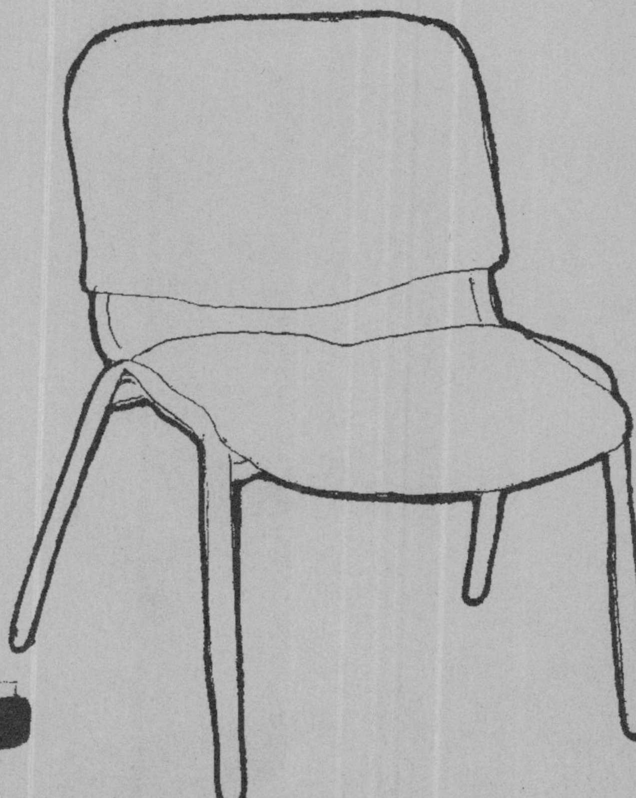

TIONAL
ES FOR
ITING
ROOM

CALL IN PSYCHIC ADVOCATE:

IMAGINE A GUARDIAN, SOMEONE YOU KNOW, AN ANCESTOR, A TEACHER, AN ACTAVIST, AUTHOR, FRIEND - WHOEVER IS A WELL OF EMOTIONAL + SPIRITUAL STRENGTH. IMAGINE THEY ARE BEHIND YOU, SUPPORTING YOU, ASK THEM TO BE THERE DURING YOUR APPOINTMENT. TRY TO CONTINUE TO FEEL A CONNECTION.

7 AWARENESS,
OR THE MIND.
ER FOR YOU
ES INCLUDE:
VDER YOU,
THE GROUND
J THE ROOM
VISUALIZE A
OR OBJECT OR
HAT FEELS SAFE
TEXTURE
YOU CAN TOUCH

BREATH:

the breath is a powerful tool, however some find it more anxiety inducing to focus on the breath. If the breath is supportive a simple breath pattern for stress is the BOX BREATH

1. breath in counting to four seconds
2. hold the breath for four seconds
3. exhale through mouth for four seconds
4. repeat steps 1-3 as needed & feels supportive

ORIGAMI

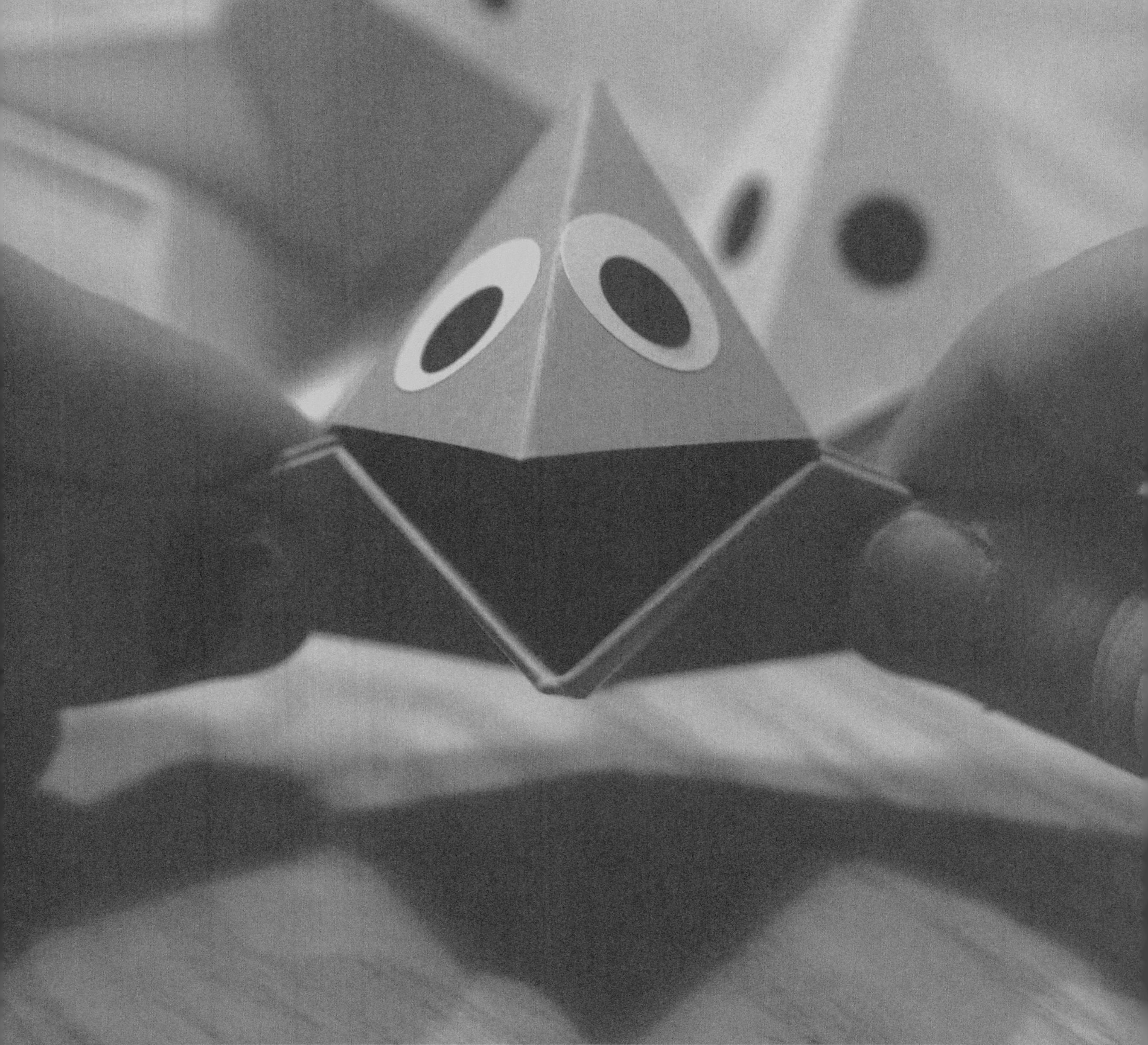

In the silence of the waiting room, I suggest you make an origami puppet using the paper on the following pages – or any other important form you've been given to fill in on arrival. My favourite is the one where you write down the name of the person you trust in case you die. The drama of this one goes perfectly with the origami and the baroque of its folds.
At the hospital, medical staff wage a fierce war against illness, even if it means silencing you. But illness is a living organism that keeps you company, with which you must communicate and negotiate if you want to achieve happiness. With this puppet, you'll finally be able to become the ventriloquist of disease. So when the endocrinologist calls you, maybe you could decide to speak only through this 'claque-bec'? And in the meantime, why don't you get your disease puppet to talk to the other beaks around you?

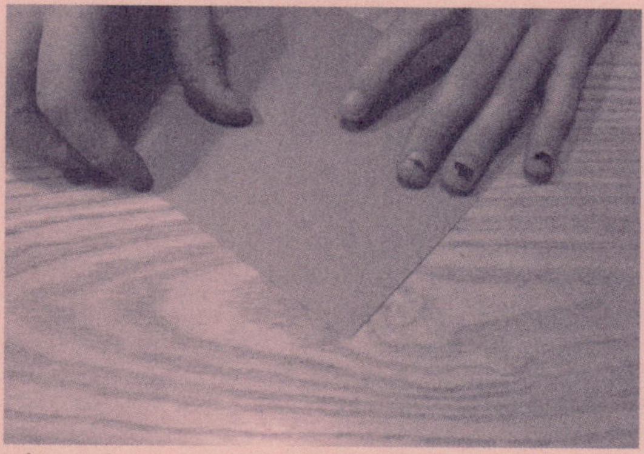

Place the square with one of the points facing up.

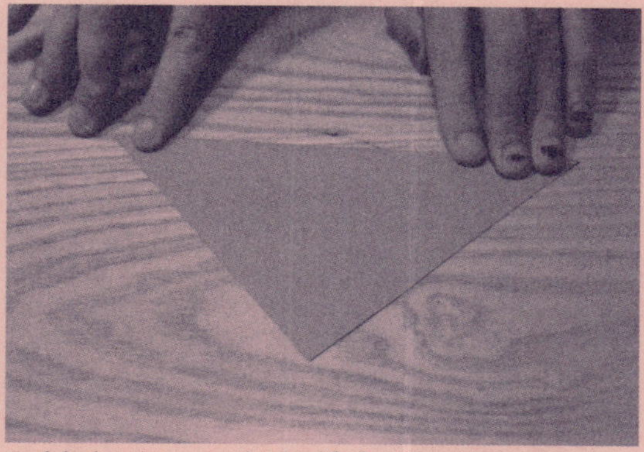

Fold the square in half, folding the side from right to left. Unfold.

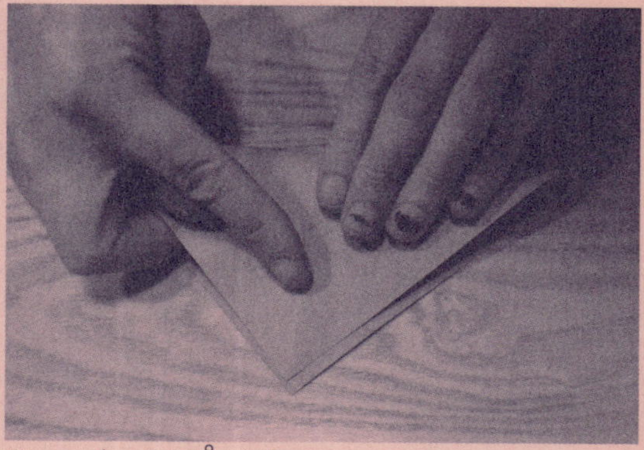

Turn sheet 45° and repeat previous step.

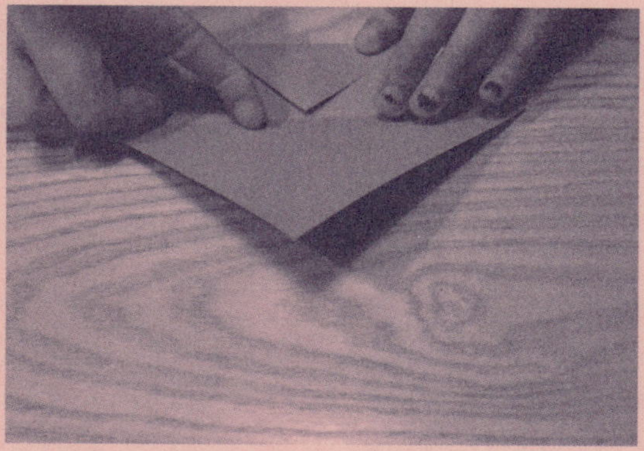

Fold the right-hand point towards the centre.

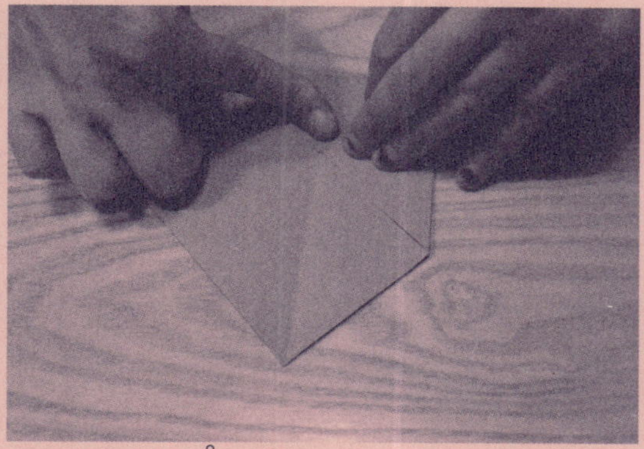

Turn sheet 45° and repeat.

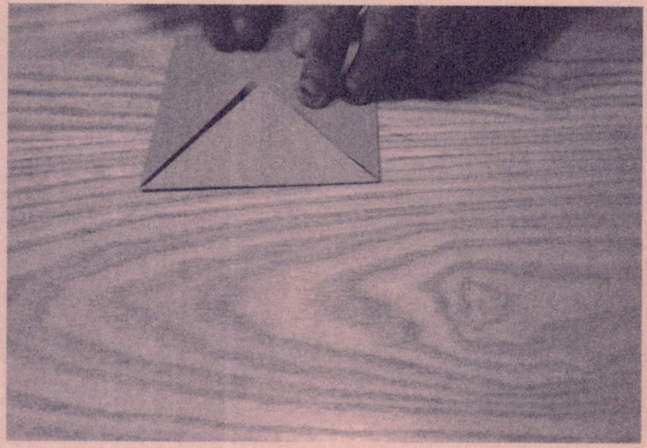

Repeat twice.

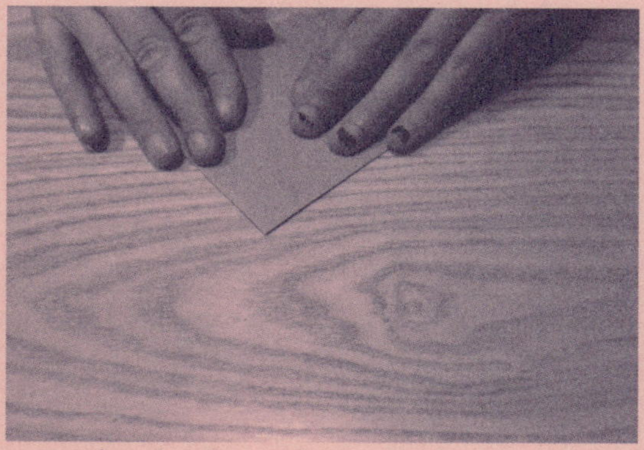

Turn the sheet upside down.

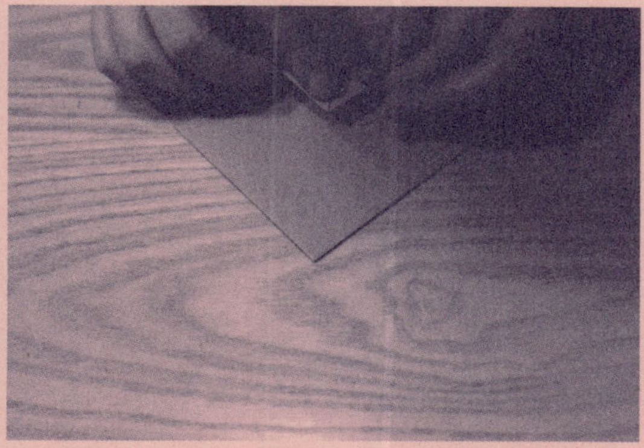

Fold the right point towards the centre.

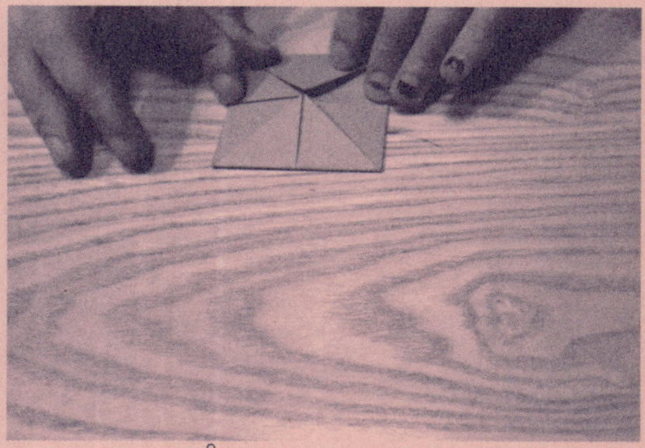

Turn sheet 45° and repeat until a new square is formed.

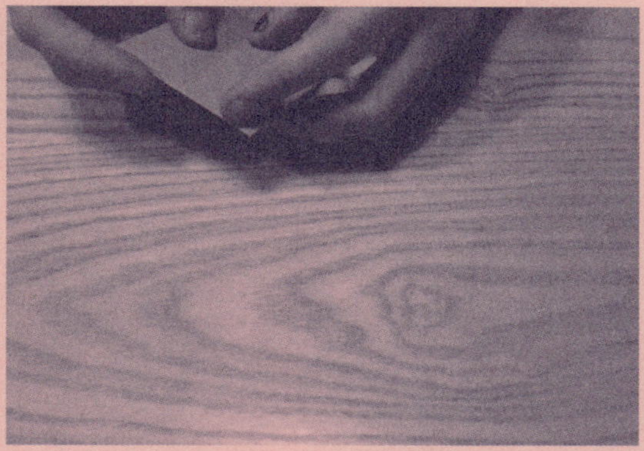

Turn the sheet over and hold it in your hand, with the opening triangle facing upwards.

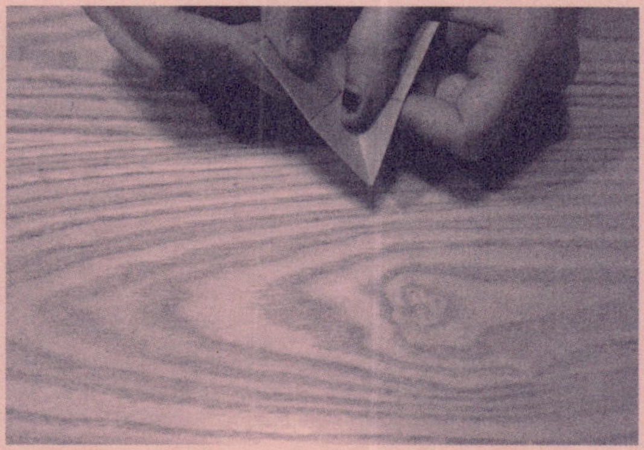

Fold in half, first one way, then the other.

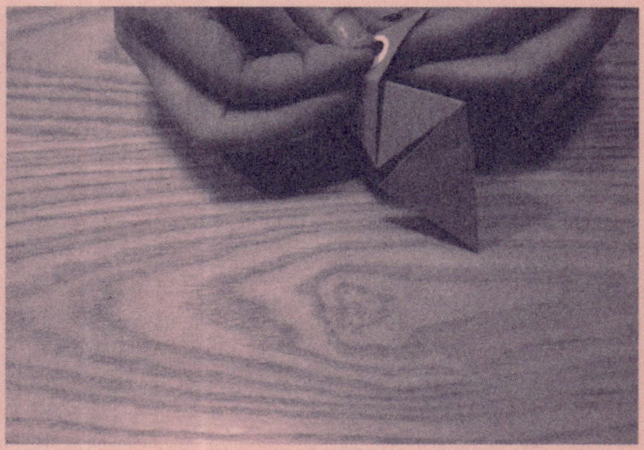

Place the eyes and slightly lift the triangle they are on.

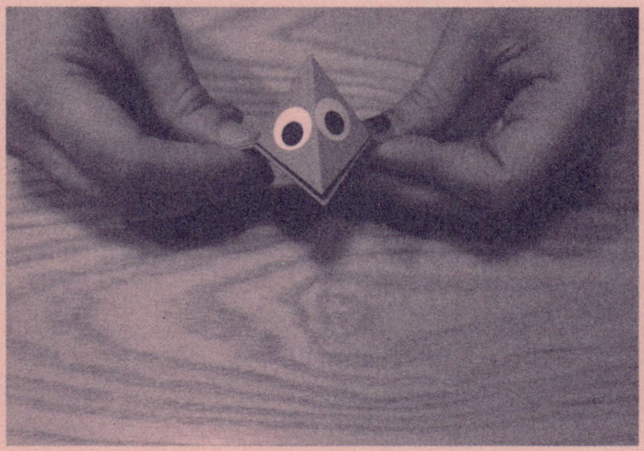

Fold the bottom towards the centre.

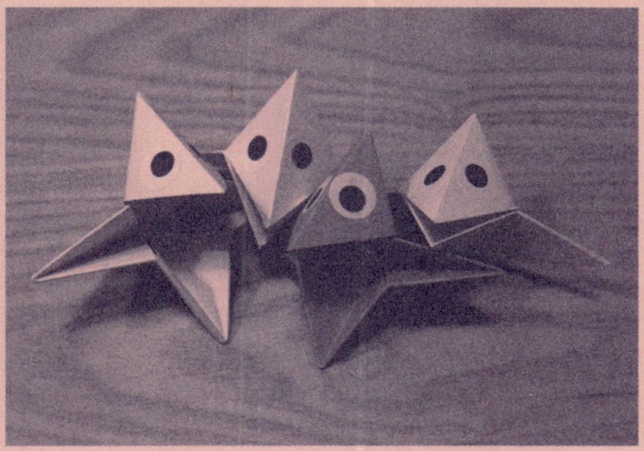

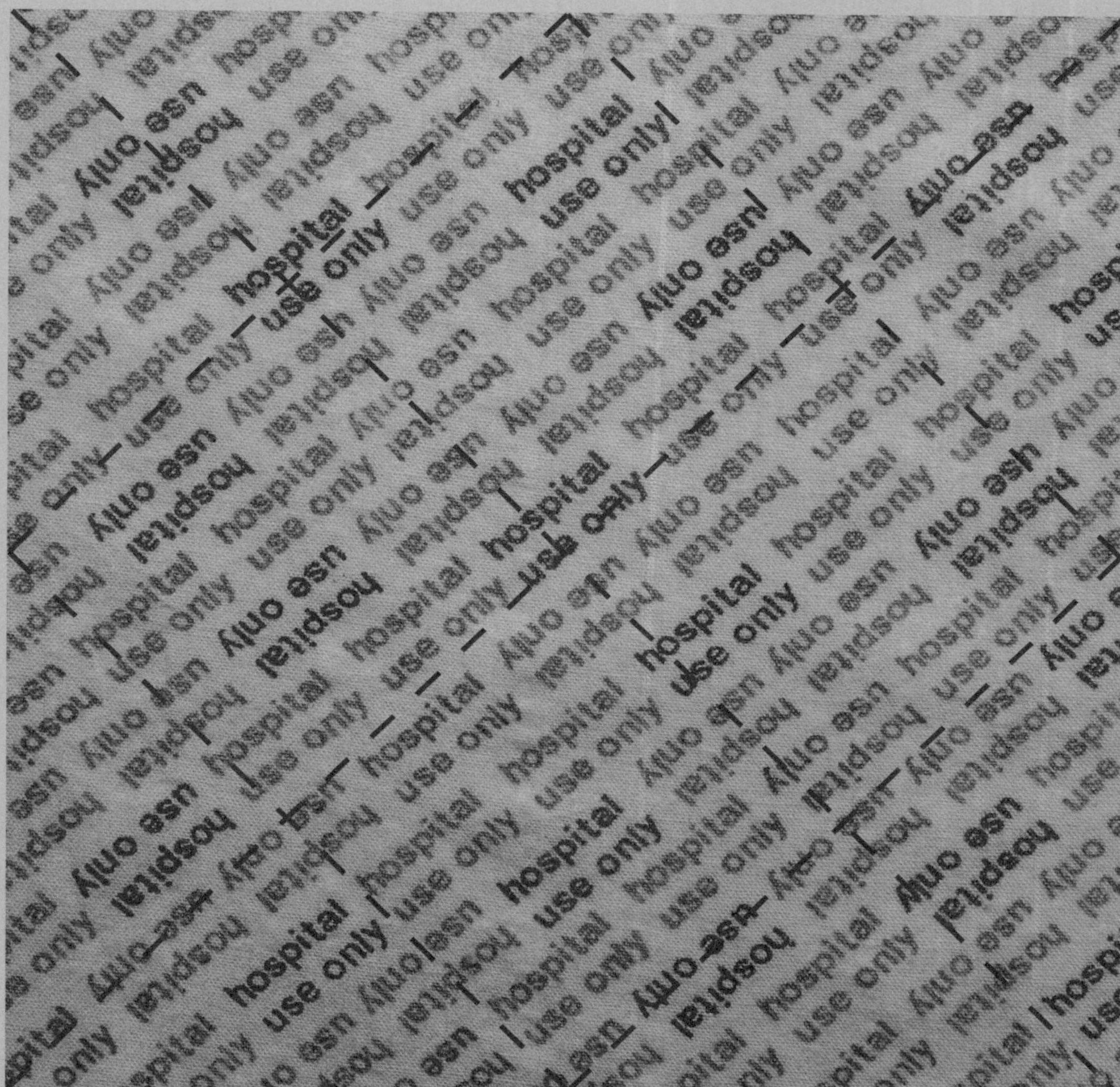
hospital
use only

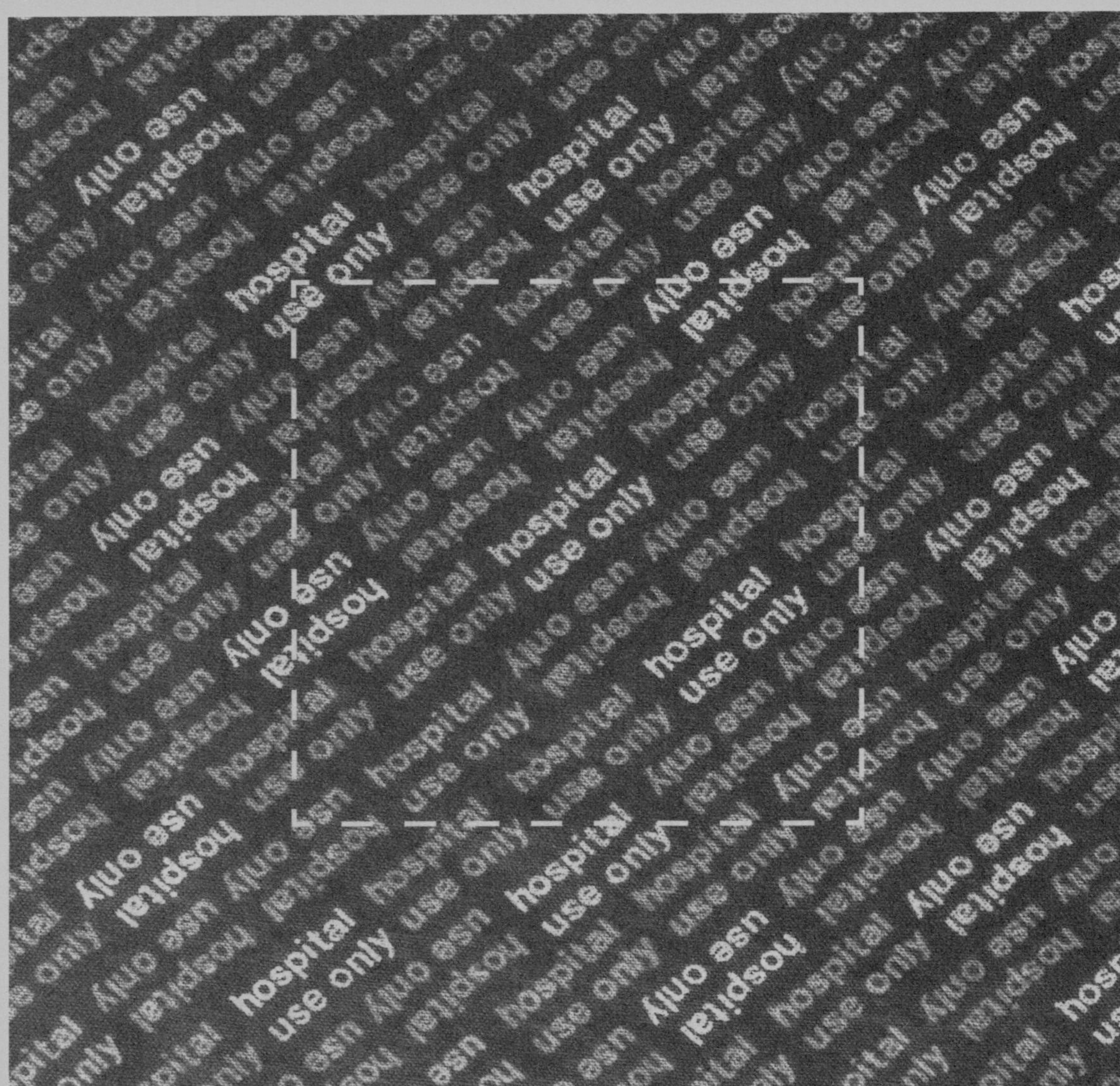
hospital
use only

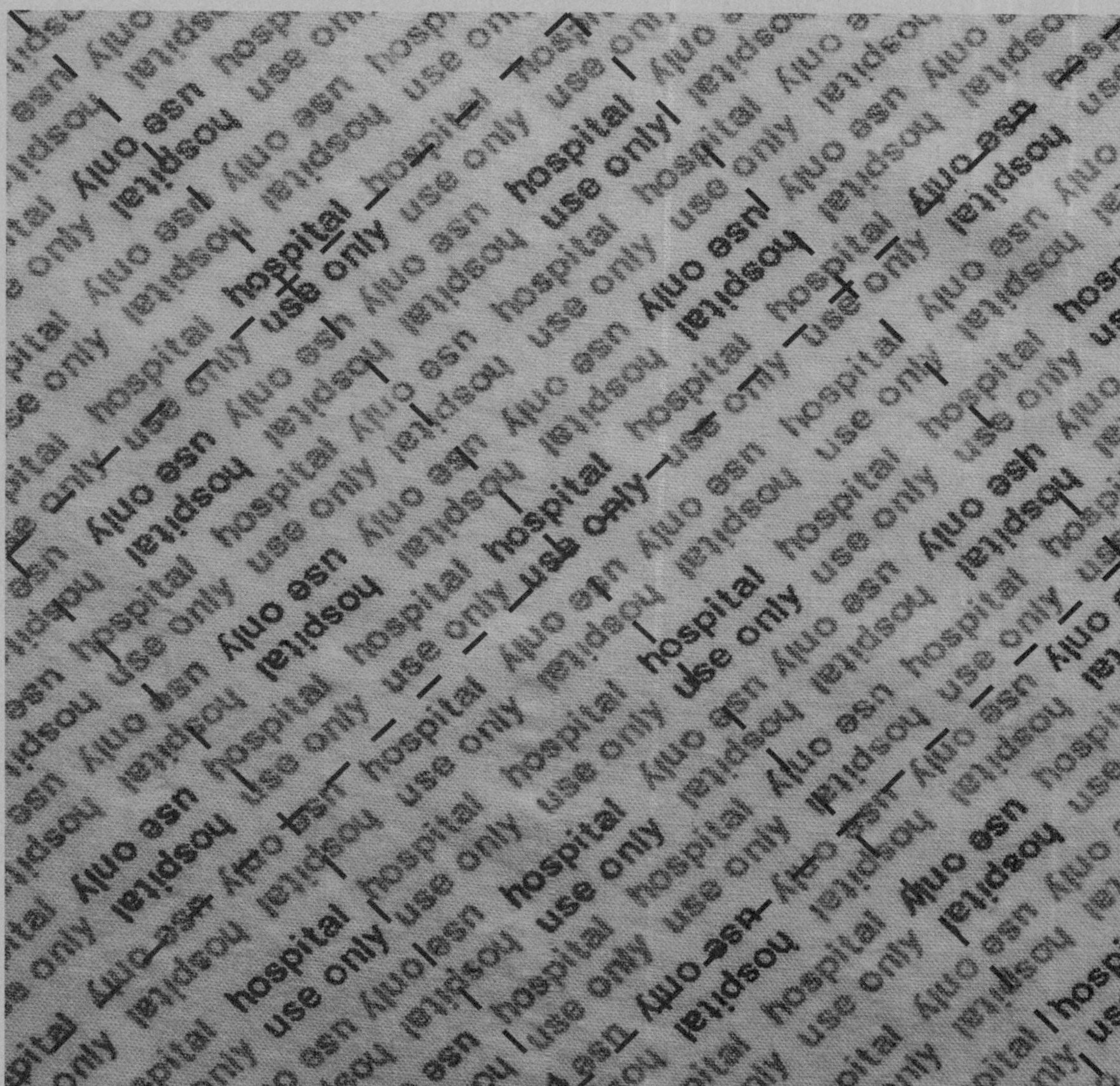
hospital
use only

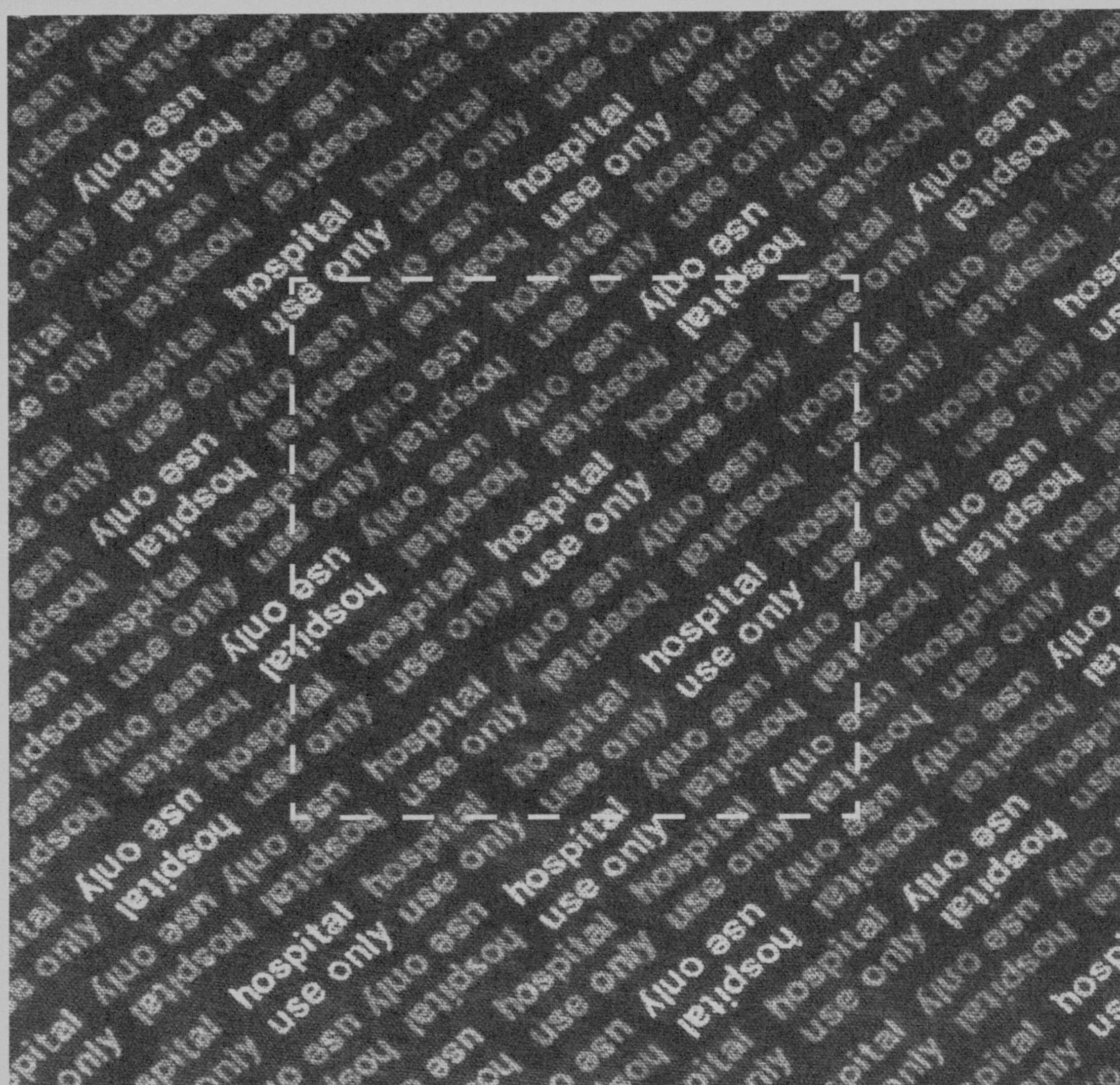
hospital
use only

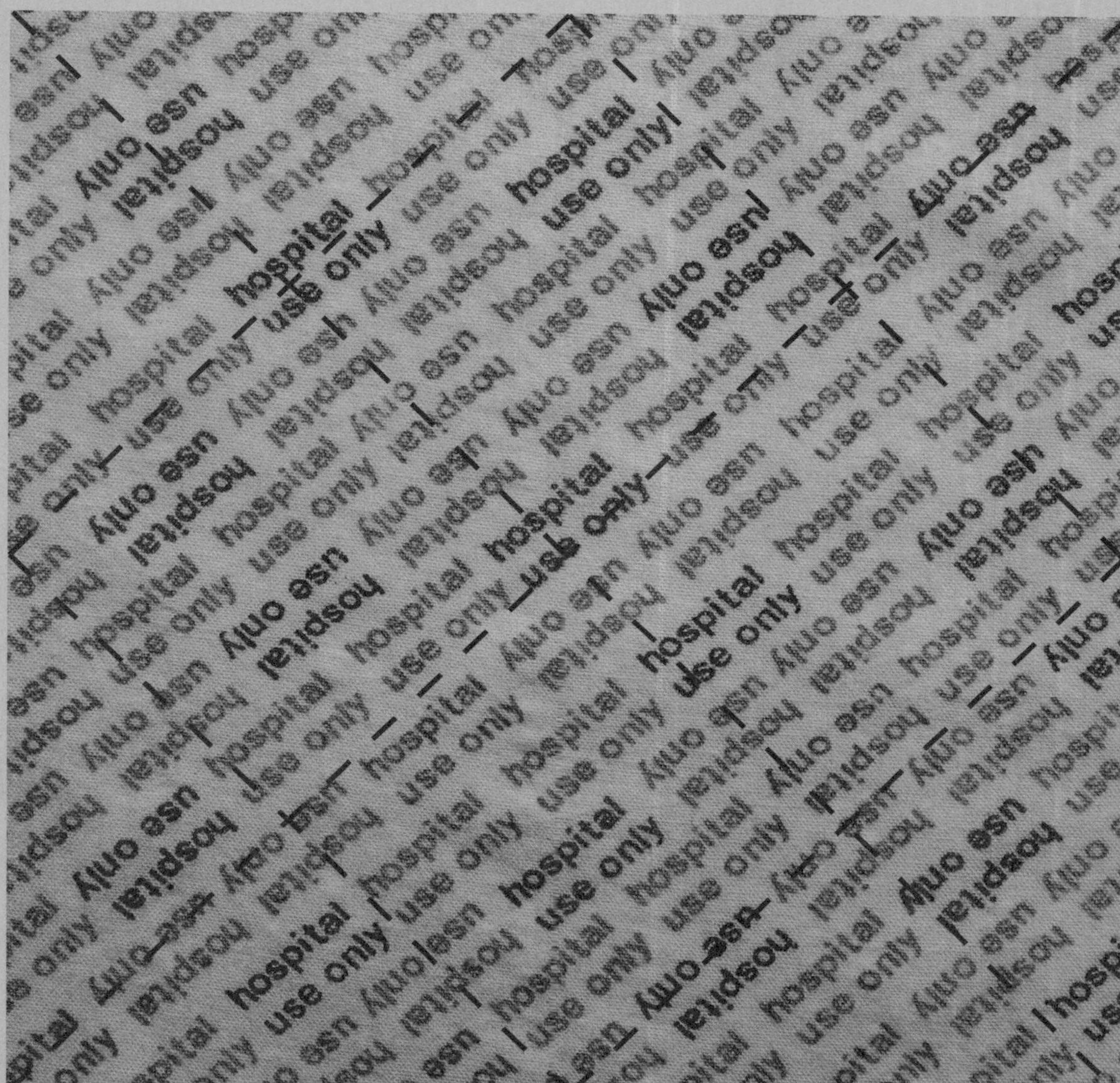
hospital
use only

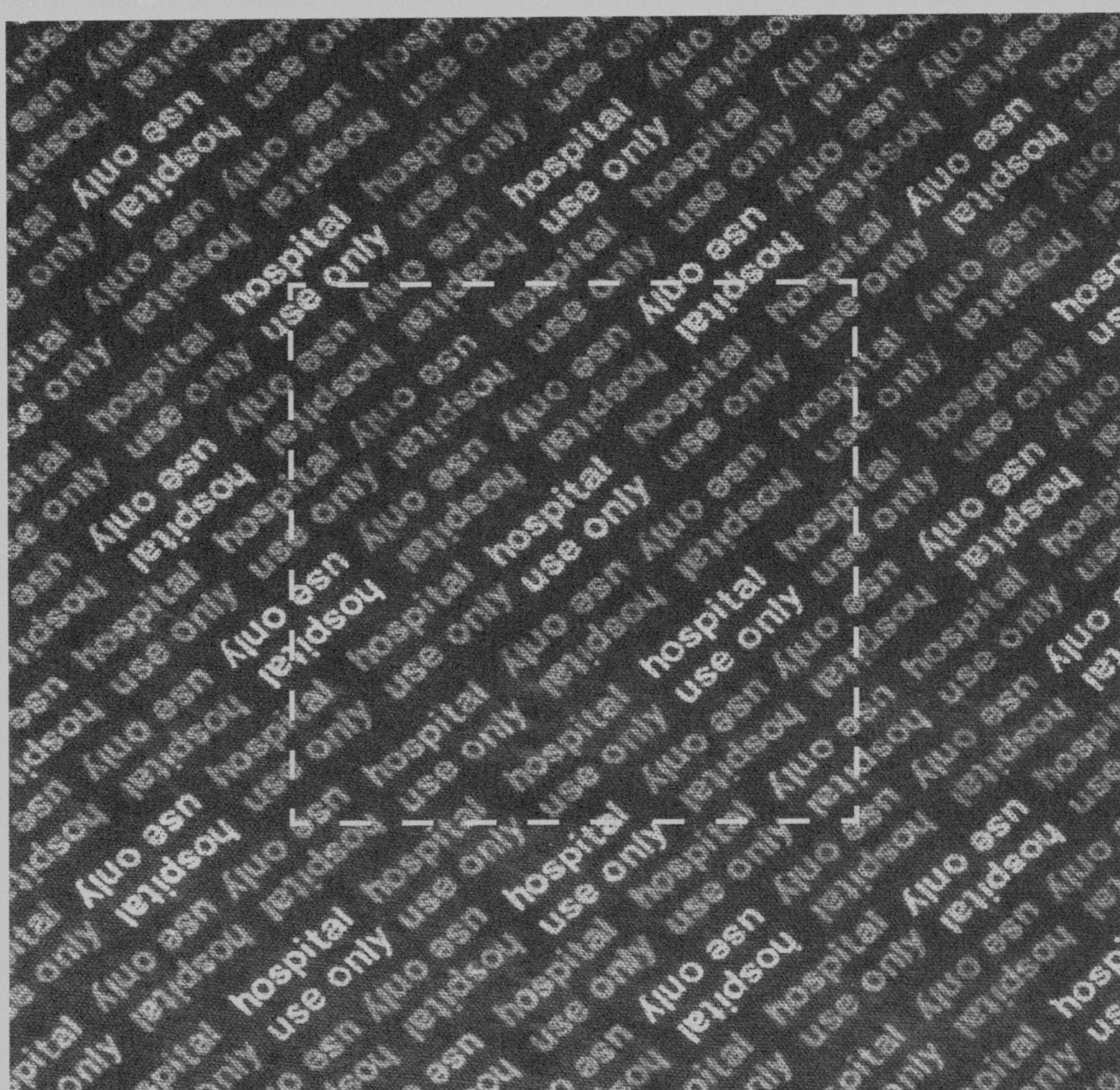
hospital
use only

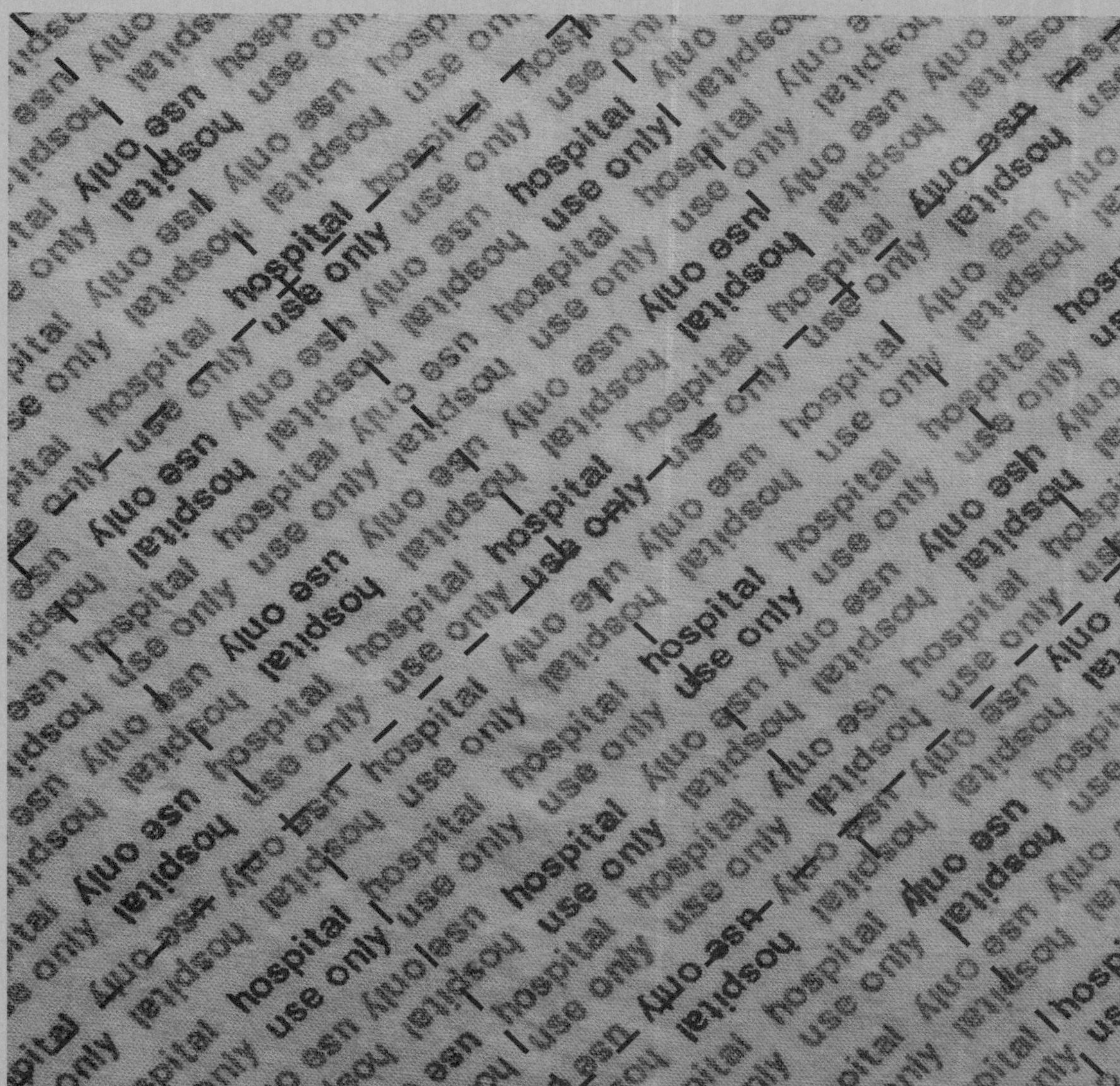
hospital
use only

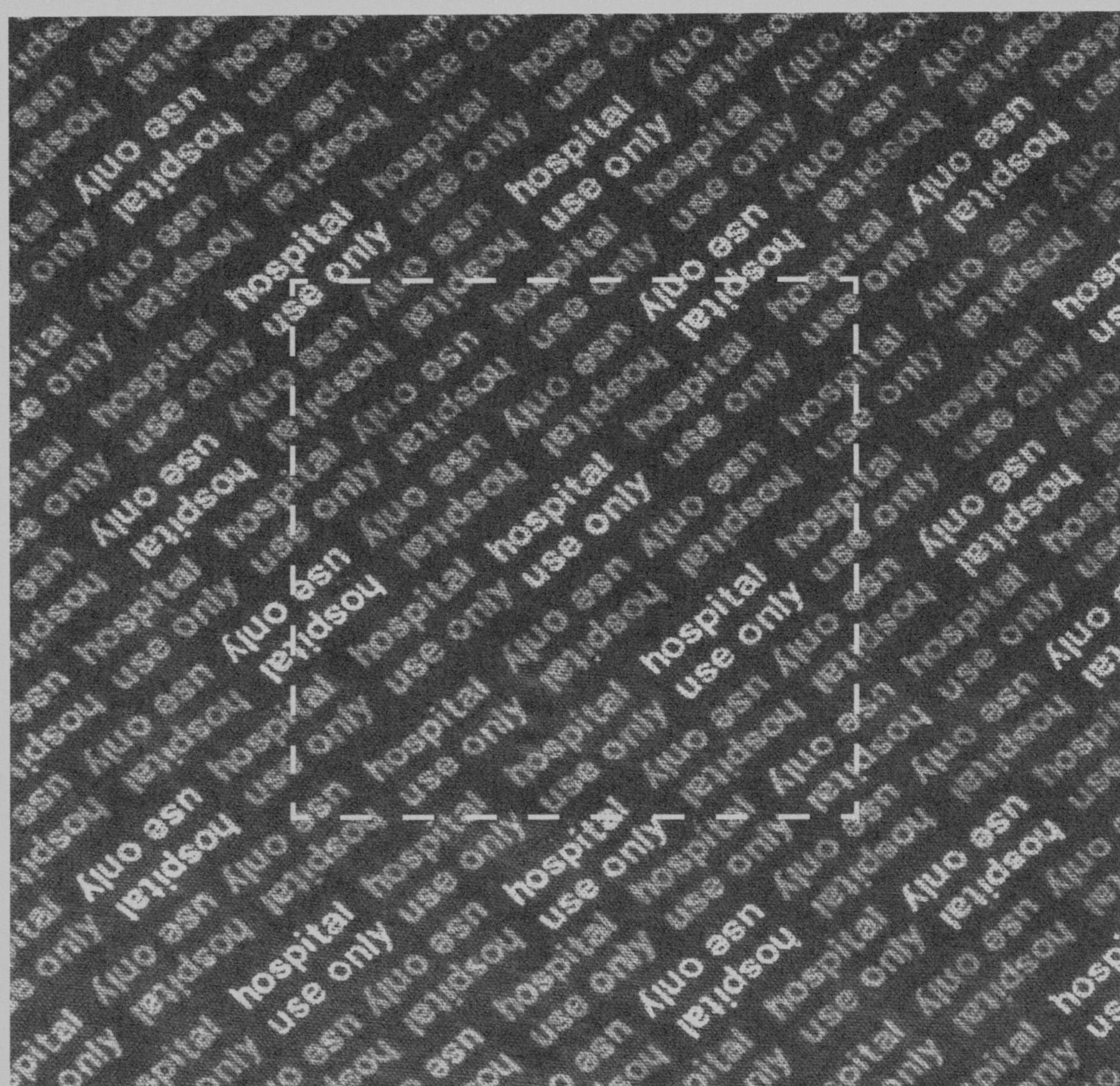
hospital
use only

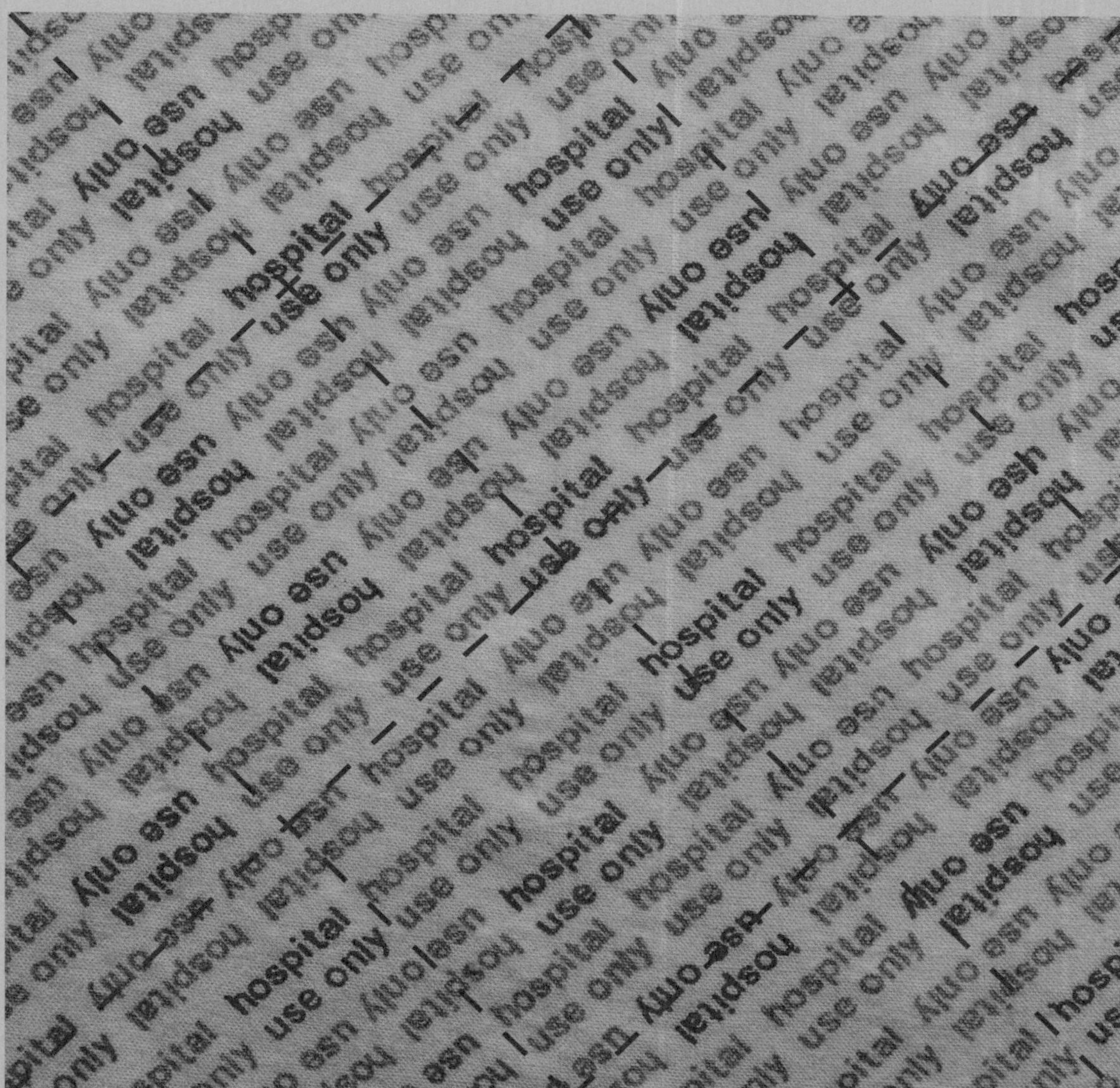
hospital
use only

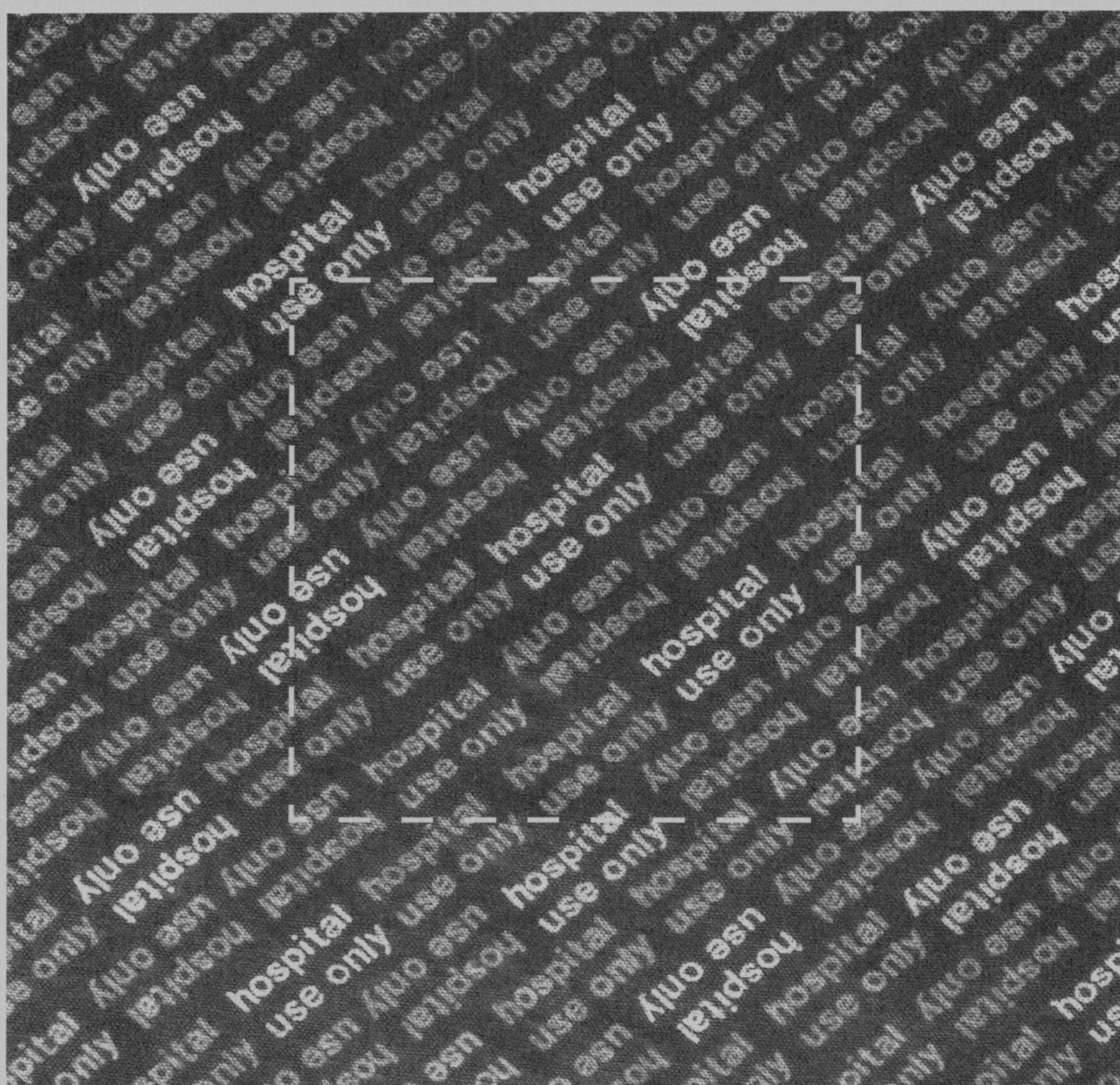
hospital
use only

BIOGRAPHIES

BENOÎT PIÉRON

Benoît Piéron lives and works in Paris, France. Selected exhibitions include: *Monstera deliciosa*, mumok, Vienna (2023); *Get Well Soon (Prologue)*, Ormston House, Limerick City (2023); *Der pinkelnde Tod or what the dead do*, Kunstverein Bielefeld (2023); *Avant l'orage*, Bourse de Commerce, Pinault Collection, Paris (2023); *uMoya: The sacred Return of Lost Things*, Liverpool Biennial (2023); *Exposé·es*, Palais de Tokyo, Paris (2023); *Illness Shower*, Sultana Summer Set, Arles (2022); *Horizones*, 23e Prix Fondation Pernod Ricard, Paris (2022); *Bandage*, Antre Peux – Haïdouc, Bourges (2022); *Deux Drapeaux, Une Belladone*, L'alcôve, Paris (2021); *VIH/sida, l'épidémie n'est pas finie!*, Mucem, Marseille (2021); *Plaid*, Cité internationale des Arts, Paris (2021); *Mort is more*, Brasserie Atlas, Brussels (2021); *Seconde peau • soft walls, patch.e.s & soap*, Cité internationale des Arts, Paris (2021). In 2022, Piéron was nominated for the Prix Fondation Pernod Ricard, The Prix Pujade-Lauraine • Carta Bianca, and was featured in ElaineAlain by ADAGP. He was previously in residence at the Pinault Collection, Lens (2022–2023) and the Cité internationale des Arts, Paris (2020). Piéron is currently in residence with Art Explora, Paris (2023–2024), and will be in residence at Les Capucins, Embrun, France, and La Becque, La Tour-de-Peilz, Switzerland (2024).

OLIVIA AHERNE

Olivia Aherne is a curator from/based in the UK, currently working as Curator at Chisenhale Gallery, London. Aherne previously worked as Curator at Nottingham Contemporary where she developed new commissions by Carolyn Lazard, Meriem Bennani and Mélanie Matranga. She's developed curatorial projects for Nir Altman, Munich (2020); Art Night, London (2019); SAFA, Shanghai; LUX Moving Image and Lewisham Arthouse, London (2018). In 2018, she was awarded the NEON Curatorial Award in partnership with the NEON Foundation and the Whitechapel Gallery, London and participated in the inaugural Shanghai Curators Lab led by Carolyn Christov-Bakargiev.

CLAY AD

Clay AD is a sentient ball of spikes, a student of the body, and lover of dirt. His practice involves making sculpture, writing, facilitating workshops, and offering somatic body-work. His work (solo, group, and workshops) has been shown at SLUG Gallery, Leipzig (2022); Tanztage Festival, Berlin (2021); *Forum: Altered States*, Kunstinstituut Melly, Rotterdam (2021); Rewire Festival, The Hague (2021); CUE Art Foundation, New York (2020); and La Casa Encendida, Madrid (2020). His first poetry book *Holy Bodies* was published with Pilot Press in 2023, and his science fiction novel *Metabolize, If Able* was published in 2018 by Monster House Press and is available as a second edition print by Arcadia Missa Publications.

PAUL MAHEKE

Paul Maheke's multidisciplinary practice spans video, installation, and sculpture through to interventions, dance, and public conversations. His work has been shown in solo presentations at High Line Art, New York (2022), The Renaissance Society, Chicago (2021); Collection Pinault, Paris (2021); Chisenhale Gallery, London (2019); Vleeshal Centre for Contemporary Art, Middelburg (2018); and South London Gallery, London (2016). He has participated in group exhibitions and festivals at institutions including ICA Miami (2019); Centre Pompidou, Paris (2018); Tate Modern, London (2017); and Serpentine Galleries, London (2016). He has been featured in major international exhibitions including Biennale du Congo, Kinshasa (2022); Glasgow International (2021); 58th Venice Biennale (2019); Baltic Triennial 13 (2018); and Manifesta 12, Palermo (2018).

ROXANNE MAILLET

Roxanne Maillet lives and works in Les Lilas, France. She is graduate of the École nationale supérieure des beaux-arts de Lyon and the ERG Brussels. Her work takes the form of group readings, publications and typographic experiments on various media. Among her projects, she initiated the *Cave Club* (2016), a recitation of texts by women that she reinterprets in writing in the form of editions, and she created *Out of Closet* (2017), textual compositions on t-shirts engaging forms of inclusive writing. Roxanne Maillet is the co-creator of the journal *Phylactère*, dealing with orality and its forms of subjective transcriptions, and she is an activist in the collective Bye Bye Binary, which militates typographically for a less binary French language.

ZOÉ WHITLEY

Dr. Zoé Whitley is Chisenhale Gallery's Director. An award-winning curator, she co-curated the acclaimed Tate Modern exhibition *Soul of a Nation: Art in the Age of Black Power* and its subsequent international tour (2017–2020). Whitley has distinguished herself working in UK institutions (2019 British Pavilion, Venice Biennale; 2014–2019 Tate Modern; 2013–2015 Tate Britain; 2003–2013 V&A), and also as a writer for all reading ages including children's titles *Meet the Artist: Frank Bowling*; *Meet the Artist: Sophie Taeuber-Arp*; and consulting for *Black Artists Shaping the World.* She is a Trustee of the Teiger Foundation and is a member of the London Mayor's Commission for Diversity in the Public Realm.

LIST OF WORKS

Benoît Piéron: Slumber Party
Chisenhale Gallery, London (2023)

Front of House
Monica
Recycled hospital gowns, cotton, glass beads & plastic. Sewing pattern courtesy of BeeZeeArt.
44 × 18 × 9 cm

Gallery
Slumber Party
Recycled hospital sheets, cotton, metal D-rings, tulip wood, matt lacquer, crepe polyester, polystyrene, paint & window film. Dimensions variable.

Radical Softness
15 emergency response lights, diffuser film, spray paint, matt lacquer & 2-core cables. Dimensions variable.

All works 2023

READING LIST

A reading list of books, articles, films, and music has been compiled in collaboration with Benoît Piéron to accompany his exhibition, *Slumber Party*, at Chisenhale Gallery. Expanding on his commission and ongoing practice, the references here consult self-published texts, feminist literature, children's stories, vampiric legends, and more. Theories of colour, references to botanical life, and the politics of textile, and their intersections with the temporality of illness, punctuate the list. Within the starkness of medical institutional frameworks, the list's meditations on bodies and time provide a gentle touch, wherein sensuality and softness become transformative agents of potential.

Almereyda, Michael, director. *Nadja*. October Films, 1994. 93 min.

Bak, Meredith A. *Playful Visions: Optical Toys and the Emergence of Children's Media Culture*. Cambridge: MIT Press, 2020.

Barthes, Roland. *The Neutral: Lecture Course at the Collège de France, 1977–1978*. Translated by Rosalind Krauss and Denis Hollier. New York City: Columbia University Press, 2005.

Berlant, Lauren. *Cruel Optimism*. Durham: Duke University Press, 2011.

Bryan-Wilson, Julia. *Fray: Art and Textile Politics*. Chicago: The University of Chicago Press, 2017.

Cluitmans, Laurie, ed. *On the Necessity of Gardening: An ABC of Art, Botany and Cultivation*. Amsterdam: Valiz, 2021.

de Maistre, Xavier. *A Journey Round My Room.* Translated by Henry Atwell. London: Longmans, Green, Reader, & Dyer, 1871.

Foster, Hal. *Design and Crime (And Other Diatribes)*. London: Verso, 2002.

Frelinghuysen, Alice Cooney. *Louis Comfort Tiffany and Laurelton Hall: An Artist's Country Estate*. New York City: Metropolitan Museum of Art, 2006.

Gandy, Matthew. *Ecologie Queer: Sexualité et Hétérotopies*. Paris: ETEROTOPIA, 2015.

Gautherot, Franck and Seungduk Kim, eds. *Pattern, Crime & Decoration.* Dijon: Les presses du réel, 2020.

Gombrich, E.H.. *The Sense of Order: A Study in the Psychology of Decorative Art*. New York City: Phaidon press, 1994.

Gonzalez-Torres, Felix. *'Untitled' (Loverboy)*, 1989. © The Felix Gonzalez-Torres Foundation.

Haraway, Donna J. *Staying with the Trouble: Making Kin in the Chthulucene*. Durham: Duke University Press, 2016.

Has, Wojciech, director. *The Hourglass Sanatorium*. Film Polski, 1973. 119 min.

Horner, W.G., Esq. 'XI. On the Properties of the Dædaleum, a New Instrument of Optical Illusion', *The London, Edinburgh, and Dublin Philosophical Magazine and Journal of Science* 4, no. 19 (January 1, 1834): 36–41. https://doi.org/10.1080/14786443408648249.

Huhtamo, Erkki. 'All the World's a Kaleidoscope: A Media Archaeological Perspective to the Incubation Era of Media Culture', *Rivista Di Estetica*, no. 55 (March 1, 2014): 139–53. https://doi.org/10.4000/estetica.982.

Independent collective. *How to Become The Daughters of Darkness*. Paris: How to Become, 2023.

Jarman, Derek. *Chroma: A Book of Colour – June '93*. London: Vintage, 1995.

Jowsey, Tanisha. 'Time and Chronic Illness: A Narrative Review', *Quality of Life Research* 25, no. 5 (October 29, 2015): 1093–1102. https://doi.org/10.1007/s11136-015-1169-2.

Kira, Alexander. *The Bathroom, Criteria for Design*. New York City: Bantam, 1966.

Kominz, David, Phyllis Damon, and David Hall. *Plastic Lace Crafts for Beginners: Groovy Gimp, Super Scoubidou, and Beast Boondoggle*. Mount Joy: Design Originals, 2013.

Leathers, Philippa. *The Black Rabbit*. London: Walker Books, 2013.

Le Fanu, Joseph Sheridan. *Carmilla*. 1871.

Meijer, Inge. *The Plant Collection*. Amsterdam: Roma Publications, 2019.

Oates, Katie. '"Tool of Enlightenment": The Dreamachine's Effects for Individual Autonomy', *Refract: An Open Access Visual Studies Journal* 1, no. 1 (2018): 88–89. doi: 10.5070/R71141450.

Rice, Anne. *The Vampire Chronicles*. New York City: Ballantine Books, 1976–2018.

Socialist Patients' Collective. *SPK: Turn Illness into a Weapon*. Translated by Huber Wolfgang. Preface by Jean-Paul Sartre. Heidelberg: KRRIM, 1993.

Sommer-Bodenburg, Angela. *The Little Vampire*. Hamburg: Rowohlt Verlag, 1979.

Sontag, Susan. *Illness as Metaphor.* New York City: Farrar, Straus and Giroux, 1978.

Starhawk. *Dreaming the Dark: Magic, Sex, and Politics.* Boston: Beacon Press, 1982.

Valadon, Suzanne. 'Obsession Magnifique (Pompidou-Metz)', 28 June 2023. http://le-beau-vice.blogspot.com/2023/06/suzanne-valadon-obsession-magnifique.html?m=1.

Wheelchair Sports Camp. 'YESS i'm a MESS', Bandcamp, single, 2021.

Wittig, Monique. *The Lesbian Body*. Translated by David Le Vay. Boston: Beacon Press, 1986.
Wittman, Mark. *Felt Time: The Psychology of How We Perceive Time*. Translated by Erik Butler. Cambridge: MIT Press, 2016.

Wright, Linda. *Toilet Paper Origami: Delight Your Guests with Fancy Folds and Simple Surface Embellishments*. Santa Barbara: Lindaloo Enterprises, 2008.

ARTIST ACKNOWLEDGEMENTS

Oscar Abdulla
Tom Adriani
Olivia Aherne
Lavendhri Arumugam
Alex Blackbourn
Georgina Corrie
Grant Foster
Lex Franchi
Hampus Hoh
Amy Jones
Rosie Kennedy
Zeynep Koksal
Paulina Michnowska
Duncan Morris
Ioanna Nitsou
Seth Pimlott
Bishwadhan Rai
Clare Rees-Hales
Sandra Ross
Josie Spalla
Emma Starkings
Rachel Be-Yun Wang
Lucy Woodhouse
Zoé Whitley
Daniel Wilkinson

Clay AD
Paul Maheke
Roxanne Maillet

Antoine Cantiny
Valentina Rosas
Guillaume Sultana
Galerie Sultana

Other People's Sculpture
Christopher MacInnes
Aneeka Makwana
Marc Ratzker
Charles Stanton-Jones

Fluxus Art Projects and
Hélène Nguyen-Ban

Colette Barbier,
Antonia Scintilla,
and Fondation Pernod Ricard

Caroline Bourgeois, Emma
Lavigne, and Pinault Collection

CHISENHALE GALLERY STAFF LIST

Oscar Abdulla, Terra Foundation Curatorial Fellow
Tom Adriani, Technician
Olivia Aherne, Curator
Lavendhri Arumugam, Operations Manager
Rachel Be-Yun Wang, Asymmetry Curatorial Research Fellow
Alex Blackbourn, Front of House and Events Coordinator
Dwayne Coleman, Technician
Georgina Corrie, Finance Manager
Grant Foster, Technician
Alessia Franchi, Technician
Hampus Hoh, Front of House and Events Assistant
Amy Jones, Associate Curator
Rosie Kennedy, Technician
Zeynep Koksal, Programme & Development Coordinator
Paulina Michnowska, Technician
Duncan Morris, Technician
Ioanna Nitsou, Head of Development
Seth Pimlott, Curator: Social Practice
Bishwadhan Rai, Participation Assistant
Clare Rees-Hales, Technician
Sandra Ross, Trusts and Foundation Manager
Josie Spalla, Digital and Communications Coordinator
Emma Starkings, Deputy Director
Zoé Whitley, Director
Daniel Wilkinson, Technician
Lucy Woodhouse, Head Technician

EXHIBITION CREDITS

Benoît Piéron: Slumber Party
Chisenhale Gallery, London
15 September–12 November 2023

Slumber Party is commissioned by Chisenhale Gallery, London and produced with support from the Chisenhale Gallery Commissions Fund.

Lead Exhibition Supporter: Fondation Pernod Ricard.
Headline Exhibition Supporter: Fluxus Art Projects, and Galerie Sultana.
With special thanks to our drinks sponsor Perrier-Jouët.

The Chisenhale Gallery Curatorial Fellowship 2023–24 is supported by the Terra Foundation for American Art.

The 2023–24 Asymmetry Curatorial Research Fellow is hosted by Chisenhale Gallery.

Fondation Pernod Ricard

Chisenhale Gallery
Registered charity number: 1026175

This book was published on the occasion of the exhibition *Benoît Piéron: Slumber Party* at Chisenhale Gallery, London

15 September—12 November 2023

CHISENHALE GALLERY

Chisenhale Gallery
64 Chisenhale Rd
Bow, London E3 5QZ
chisenhale.org.uk

Edited by
Zoé Whitley
Amy Jones

Managing Editor
Amy Jones

Assistant Editor
Oscar Abdulla

Publishing Editor, Mousse
Micola Clara Brambilla

Graphic design, Mousse
Gloria Favaro

Copy editing and proofreading
Lindsey Westbrook
Rachel Be-Yun Wang
Emma Passarella

Texts
Clay AD
Olivia Aherne
Paul Maheke
Benoît Piéron
Zoé Whitley

Activities
Clay AD
Paul Maheke
Roxanne Maillet
Benoît Piéron

Printed by
Grafiche Zanini, Bologna

First edition 2023

pp. 26–55
Slumber Party installation views by Andy Keate, 2023. Courtesy of Chisenhale Gallery, London.

pp. 58–72
Photo: Benoît Piéron

The Waiting Room Activities were commissioned for the publication *Benoît Piéron: Slumber Party*

pp. 80–81
Paul Maheke, *ODDOWL* (2023)

pp. 82–83
Roxanne Maillet, *A Queer History of Flowers* (2023)

pp. 84–85
Clay AD, *Meditational Strategies for the Waiting Room* (2023)

pp. 86–98
Benoît Piéron, *Origami* (2023)

ISBN 978-88-6749-604-4

£ 23 / € 27 / $ 30

A Chisenhale Gallery Book

Published by
Mousse Publishing
Contrappunto s.r.l.
via Pier Candido Decembrio 28
20137, Milan–Italy

Available through
Mousse Publishing, Milan
moussemagazine.it
DAP | Distributed Art Publishers, New York
artbook.com
Idea Books, Amsterdam
ideabooks.nl
Les presses du réel, Dijon
lespressesdureel.com
Antenne Books, London
antennebooks.com
Motto, Berlin
mottodistribution.com
Libro Co. Italia, Firenze
libroco.it

A catalogue record for this book is available from The British Library, London.

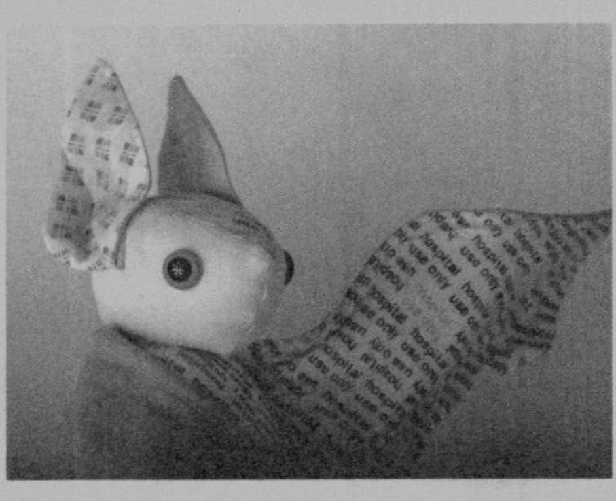